Real SMALL GROUPS

GROUPS

DON'T JUST

HAPPEN

NEAL F. McBRIDE

Real SMALL GROUPS DON'T JUST HAPPEN

Nurturing
Relationships
in your
Small Group

NAVPRESS

BRINGING TRUTH TO LIFE
NavPress Publishing Group
P.O. Box 35001, Colorado Springs, Colorado 80935

The Navigators is an international Christian organization. Our mission is to reach, disciple, and equip people to know Christ and to make Him known through successive generations. We envision multitudes of diverse people in the United States and every other nation who have a passionate love for Christ, live a lifestyle of sharing Christ's love, and multiply spiritual laborers among those without Christ.

NavPress is the publishing ministry of The Navigators. NavPress publications help believers learn biblical truth and apply what they learn to their lives and ministries. Our mission is to stimulate spiritual formation among our readers.

© 1998 by Neal F. McBride
Library of Congress Catalog Card Number: 98-16991
ISBN 1-57683-103-5

Some of the anecdotal illustrations in this book are true to life and are included with the permission of the persons involved. All other illustrations are composites of real situations, and any resemblance to people living or dead is coincidental.

Unless otherwise identified, all Scripture quotations in this publication are taken from the *New American Standard Bible* (NASB), © The Lockman Foundation 1960, 1962, 1963, 1968, 1971, 1972, 1973, 1975, 1977.

McBride, Neal.
     Real small groups don't just happen: nurturing relationships in your small group/Neal F. McBride.
          p. cm.
     ISBN 1-57683-103-5 (pbk.)
     1. Church group work. 2. Small groups. 3. Christian leadership I. Title.
BV 652.2.M37 1998
253'.7--dc21   98-16991
                                                                                                              CIP

Printed in the United States of America

1 2 3 4 5 6 7 8 9 10 11 12 13 14 15 / 05 04 03 02 01 00 99 98

Contents

Introduction		9
ONE	All Groups Aren't Really Groups	11
TWO	Tour Guide, You're Vital	17
THREE	Pre-Trip Preparation	33
FOUR	We're Off	47
FIVE	The Journey's Challenges	63
SIX	Almost There	75
SEVEN	Arriving at the Destination	91
EIGHT	Heading Home	109
NINE	Tour Celebration	125
TEN	Trip Strategies	135
Recommended Resource List		151

5.55

95886

To my parents Merle and Louise McBride
To my in-laws Louis and Vera Buchanan

Introduction

Welcome! Did you know all groups are alike, but no two are the same? Please excuse my apparent contradiction in words, yet it's a fact: All groups are similar and at the same time unique. How so? Simple — like people, each group shares common characteristics true for all groups, while expressing its own identity and personality. For example, my daughter, Katie, is a young woman with a unique physical identity and personality. She has similar attributes and characteristics associated with many other women. As is the case with groups, I can highlight her uniqueness while describing the attributes she shares in common with other women.

Real Small Groups Don't Just Happen is for anyone who works with groups, especially if you are involved with group ministries within your church. The goal is to help you understand your group's uniqueness by presenting various characteristics common to all groups. Together we'll explore the inner workings of groups so you in turn can assist your group in its journey toward becoming a full-fledged, functioning, effective group.

Most people working with groups receive little or no training in how to lead a group, let alone any instruction on a group's human inter-workings or relational dynamics. How about you? What training did you receive prior to becoming a group leader? Regardless of your background, this book is intended to provide you with some foundational and practical knowledge — even a few functional skills — you need to lead and assist your group in its formation.

By now you may be getting the idea that this book is about group dynamics. Well, it is, sort of. It focuses on the human aspects within small groups. However, our journey together deals more with applied group dynamics than with explanations of technical or theoretical issues. Likewise, I don't spend much time discussing group organization or administrative details. My intent is to describe the human conditions and situations associated with effective group cultivation and operation. Such information will, hopefully, alert you to various personal and interpersonal dynamics at work in your group and provide valuable insights on how your group develops, functions, and accomplishes its objectives.

CHAPTER ONE

All Groups Aren't Really Groups

Take your stand with God's loyal community and live,
or chase after phantoms of evil and die.
Proverbs 11:19, *The Message*

READY for a real pearl of wisdom? Not all groups are really groups. Some are merely a collection of individuals with the appearance of a group. Don't get alarmed. Rarely is this situation intentional, yet it's more common than you think. Is your group *really* a group?

Unfortunately, too many groups fail to realize the considerable benefits associated with "groupness." There are far more reasons than I can list here, but in my experience, one basic fact stands apart—the group blunders along without taking the necessary, intentional steps needed to become a true group. The members assume that by calling themselves a group, they become one. No effort is invested in taking the required steps to establish and maintain a functioning group.

Becoming a group is an intentional *process*. Rarely does a group coalesce instantly. It normally takes focused effort over a period of time. The amount of time and effort varies, but you can be certain it's more likely to happen if you consciously nurture the process along. This responsibility falls on you as the group's leader, especially early in the group's existence. All the group members must participate at some level, but as the leader you set the pace. This book is designed to set forth such a process. However, since each person reading this volume represents a unique situation, my goal is to outline a generic process you're encouraged to tailor to your group's specific needs.

Basic Principle: Rarely do groups just happen—they are most effectively created by following a defined, systematic process.

In helping you develop a systematic approach suitable for your group, I offer no simple panaceas. There are no easy, one-two-three formulas I can share with you that guarantee absolute success. Yet I do provide some general guidelines worth considering. My goal is to set forth constructive ideas that provide a productive path for you to follow. With prayer, hard work, and a few mistakes along the way, you *can* succeed in helping your group develop into a highly beneficial experience for all the members.

WHEN IS A GROUP A GROUP?

Because this book is aimed at helping your group become a real group, it's sensible to define or perhaps describe this thing we call a group. By doing so you'll have a better idea of what you're aiming at as a group leader. Several workable defining strategies are possible.

In my previous books (see Recommended Resource List) I define a group as follows:

A small group within the church is a voluntary, intentional gathering of from three to twelve people regularly meeting together with the shared goal of mutual Christian edification and fellowship.

The above definition is useful to understand the nature and purposes associated with groups in a local church context, and we will consider it again in chapter 10. But it isn't a totally adequate definition to determine or identify the inherent characteristics that mark a group in general. A more generic definition or description is needed.

Defining a group isn't as easy as it may appear. Many alternatives are possible. In fact, experts in the field offer numerous definitions depending on their particular emphasis or theoretical orientation. So, rather than attempting to provide a traditional definition, allow me to suggest seven characteristics, which I argue must be present for a group to be considered a "real" group.

1. Perception—Individual members perceive themselves as

group members. This initial and very basic characteristic is vital. The group takes its first step toward being an actual group when the individual members begin describing themselves as members and also acknowledging the group's corporate existence. Put simply, it's hard to call a group a group until the so-called members acknowledge the group's existence and their membership.

2. Motivation—A genuine group is made up of individuals who not only acknowledge their group membership, but also want to be together and function as a group. This motivation varies among the individual group members, but ideally all the members demonstrate an increasing desire to participate in the group's identity and functions.

3. Interaction—Interaction among the group members is an essential characteristic. This interaction is frequently called group communication, and numerous books are available on the subject. A real group enjoys free and open interaction among its members, even though there may be some bumpy roads along the way.

4. Duration—A genuine group meets more than once. Meetings occur frequently over a period of time. In some cases the frequency and duration are fixed; other times they may be open-ended. How often the group meets and over what period of time are critical factors for facilitating the other six characteristics in this list. In short, it takes time for the group to become a group.

5. Structure—Internal organizational structure must exist within the group. Some groups are highly organized, while others possess minimal structure. Nevertheless, a real group has some level of structure—leadership, membership requirements, covenant, and so on—to organize its functioning. It's important the chosen structure is agreed upon and understood by all the group members.

6. Purpose—Why does the group exist? Members in a genuine group are able to state the reason for meeting. Becoming a group, however, is rarely given as the group's primary purpose. Usually the group has some other objective, functional reason for meeting. For instance, a Bible study, support group, task-oriented group, or some other application is usually the group's primary purpose. Unfortunately, a group often overlooks functional group dynamics and concentrates only on its central purpose. While normal, this mistake often results in a group failing to become a group and, consequently, failing to achieve its primary purpose.

7. Size—One final characteristic is essential to consider—size. In this book we are talking about "small groups," which include between three and twelve persons. Yet, this important distinction isn't always necessary for groups in general. A group may be much larger than twelve members. However, group size—a small group—is an extremely important distinction. For more complete information on this characteristic, please refer to *How to Build a Small Groups Ministry* or *How to Lead Small Groups* (see Recommended Resource List).

Ideally, all seven characteristics exist at their peak levels. But in reality, this rarely occurs. More often than not, a group is strong in a few areas, adequate in others, and weak in one or two. Your goal as the leader is to assist the group in recognizing *all* the characteristics and attaining a workable balance. As you can surmise, neglecting even one or two puts the group's future at risk.

Groups come in all different shapes and sizes. The seven characteristics are applicable to most group situations you may encounter. In fact, I cannot think of a single group context where these characteristics are not relevant. Consequently, they provide a useful framework to guide our thinking in this book; they are the characteristics we are attempting to identify and nurture within the groups you and I lead. Even so, I need to point out some limitations or restrictions.

First, our focus is on groups in which the members are average teens or adults who already possess some ability, or are able to develop the skills necessary, to function in a group setting. Second, I assume you as the group leader, or potential leader, are not a professionally trained group facilitator. Your interest in groups is based on your prior experience in groups or your concern for ministering to people in a group setting.

Given our two restrictions, therapy groups—groups designed to counsel persons in a group context—are not discussed. Such groups share some similarities with the kinds of groups we are dealing with in this book, but they also have significant differences. Two key differences make therapy groups a discussion for another time: (1) the need for a trained professional leader and (2) the group's primary reason for existing—resolving the members' individual as well as mutual problems. I could cite other theoretical distinctions, but these two reasons alone cause us to exclude therapy groups from our present discussion.

One final thought about when a group is a real group: Groups are dynamic and require concentrated effort. Failure to recognize this fact frequently dooms the group to unnecessary struggles and perhaps even to breakdown and collapse. I'm not trying to alarm you but to forewarn you. Starting and running a group entails more than merely scheduling a time and inviting your friends to join. On the other hand, conducting a group is not like brain surgery, demanding years of education and practice. With God's help, you can succeed!

HELPING YOUR GROUP BECOME A GROUP: THE "TOUR" OR "JOURNEY"

Okay, by now you realize that becoming a group is an intentional, orderly process. To describe this process, in this book I utilize a simple but effective analogy—a tour or journey. This makes sense to me because our groups are on a journey toward becoming real groups, regardless of the specific purpose for which they exist. In this book we set off on a journey to explore group development. My role is to serve as your tour guide, and you in turn serve as your group's guide.

OUR TOUR GUIDELINES

Every tour brochure I've ever seen includes some fine print: the rules or guidelines governing the trip. Our journey toward "groupness" is no different. Here are some things to organize your thinking about our journey together:

1. The journey analogy used in this book is just that, an analogy, and as such it can break down. On occasion it may seem like I'm stretching a point a bit too much. Don't worry, I won't do it very often.
2. Everyone is invited on our journey; no one is excluded. Whether you're a novice or a highly experienced group leader, this volume provides valuable facts and insights you will likely find useful. But feel free to pick and choose. My experience and advice may or may not fit your specific situation. Only you can determine if my suggestions are suitable for your group.

3. It's okay to stop and rest as often as you like. Our journey together isn't a forced march. No one is in a rush. In fact, you may find it preferable to extend your reading over several weeks or months, thus allowing time to ponder and apply the information as you go. Short trips often are preferred to marathon journeys, which leave you tired and worn out. Getting to your destination—a successful group—is more important than the time you must spend traveling.

4. A few mistakes along the way are acceptable. Any journey has its share of wrong turns and getting lost. Count on it. My encouragement to you is straightforward: Don't get upset when it happens, just learn from your errors and don't journey down that path again. In one or two instances you might even have to apologize to your group members. Some journeys are harder than others. As you become a more experienced traveler, your error rate will diminish significantly.

To help you in your journey, at the end of each subsequent chapter I provide a "Taking Action" section. As you complete each chapter, please invest a few minutes and complete the questions or activities. In a way, it can become your travel diary. Have fun with this.

CHAPTER TWO

Tour Guide, You're Vital

Good-tempered leaders invigorate lives;
they're like spring rain and sunshine.
Proverbs 16:15, *The Message*

S EVERAL years ago my family and I went on a tour to Israel. Having never been to the Holy Land, our eagerness to go was greatly increased by the fact that we were traveling with a highly experienced guide who had already led fifty similar tours. Our confidence to journey into unfamiliar territory was bolstered by his honed leadership.

As a group leader, there are various ways to view your role — as the group's facilitator, coach, adviser, counselor, or whatever. This chapter explores your role as the group's "tour guide." It's a fun and different way to look at your leadership role. As the group's guide, you're asking the members to join you on an exciting journey . . . a journey toward becoming and functioning as a small group. Hold on, it's an exhilarating trip for both you and your group.

I cover the issues related to being a group leader fairly well in *How to Lead Small Groups* (see Recommended Resource List). So, in the upcoming pages my aim is to further develop your understanding about this vital role.

EVERY TRIP NEEDS A GOOD TOUR GUIDE

As you can imagine, traveling with an excellent tour guide makes a big difference. If you've ever been on a trip with a poor guide you know what I mean. A qualified, enthusiastic guide makes the trip much easier and far more enjoyable.

As their designated leader — their tour guide — you play a vital
role in assuring the group's productive journey. Moreover, your guidance isn't optional; I suggest it's absolutely necessary. It's the rare
group that reaches its destination without a leader. In my experience,
the bottom line is extremely clear: Every group must have a leader.
Of course, the leadership function varies in form and degree from
one group to the next, but in all cases the tour guide plays a necessary, critical role. You, as their leader, are probably the most important ingredient in the group's potential success.

Some people argue a group can function without a designated
leader. Perhaps, but I'm doubtful. The only time I've ever seen it
work, and then only to a limited degree, was when the members were
highly experienced with groups and worked hard at not having a
leader — at least by title. I recall being a member in one such group.
The other members thought having a leaderless group was a great
idea. Everyone had been in numerous groups and felt a formal, designated leader was unnecessary. I went along with the idea because I
was curious to see if it would work. Well, it worked for a few months,
but lo and behold, as time went on, one individual slowly assumed
more and more of the leadership functions. This person never had the
title "leader," but ultimately everyone came to accept and refer to
him as our group's leader.

At the risk of sounding redundant, I'll repeat myself: *Every
group needs a leader*, a good leader. The leadership role is not
optional. Groups without a designated leader are doomed almost
certainly to either ineffectiveness or plain and simple failure. I know
this sounds harsh, but it's the truth. Hopefully, you get my point by
now: Your role as the group leader is crucial to your group's overall
success. So, to help you gain further perspective on what it means to
be a good tour guide, let's move on and explore your general
responsibilities.

Tour guides serve specific purposes; they assist the group by
providing various services or performing required tasks. While this
entire book is aimed at helping you assist your group in becoming a
group, let me summarize your important role as the group's guide by
introducing you to some general tour guide responsibilities.

Be dependable—Every group depends on its leader, especially
at first. I remember how much my family and I relied on our tour

guide. Your group is no different. They place a lot of confidence and trust in you to help them get started and function as a group. This needn't be a worry for you — you can do it! Just make certain you understand your role, prepare yourself for your leadership responsibilities, and depend on the Holy Spirit.

As your group develops over time, the members' reliance on you should diminish. But it never disappears completely; it merely takes on different characteristics and responsibilities. I recall how my family was nervous when we first began our trip. We relied heavily on our guide. But as our tour proceeded, we gained considerable confidence as travelers. We still needed the tour guide, but our dependence on him declined, and we were able to do many things for ourselves.

Your success as the "designated" leader — the person everyone accepts as the group's recognized leader — is in part judged by your ability to move the group away from being too dependent on you. Groups that remain highly dependent on their leader never really seem to make it. Ultimately, your group must become responsible for itself. It's a process similar to human development. At some point, every individual must become an independent person, but this doesn't require isolation or giving up beneficial relationships. As the tour guide, you're always there to provide the group with guidance and direction when needed.

In some ways the group's reliance on you mirrors a parent-child relationship. Your task is to facilitate and guide the group toward becoming fully mature. But unlike the normal parental role, you function as an equal, a fellow group member, not as a grownup who always knows best. You aren't instructing children. You must treat the group members as intelligent adults and recognize their right to make decisions or perhaps do things you advise against. Being a group leader is *not* an authority trip, but a journey based on service and positive influence. You are a servant-leader.

Answer questions — Questions, questions! Inexperienced travelers usually are filled with questions. Likewise, group members may have numerous questions, especially those who are new to small group ministries. Don't be surprised when you find yourself being asked all sorts of relevant and irrelevant questions. It's a small part of your job.

Being the "answer man" (or woman, as the case may be) isn't

your main task and needn't be overwhelming. Hopefully, you already know the answer to many questions thrown at you. Still, when a question does stump you, be quick to respond, "I don't know, but I'll find an answer for you." Group members appreciate your honesty. After all, they know you don't know everything there is to know. There's no need to pretend you do.

The more you learn about and are involved with groups, the more you'll find answering questions an enjoyable experience. Everyone likes to be an expert in some area. I encourage you to invest the time and effort necessary to become an expert on small group ministries. Who knows how God will use you now or in the future as His small groups spokesperson? I'm amazed at how God has given me the privilege and opportunity to serve the body of Christ through my writing and speaking on the topic.

 Set the tempo— Among your tasks as the group leader, especially when the group is first beginning, is setting the tempo within the group. By "setting the tempo" I mean you are responsible for nurturing the group's atmosphere, mood, climate, pace, and so on. Similar to any tour guide, you want to make the journey enjoyable and productive. To do this, your words and actions must model the attitudes and actions you hope the group will adopt as their own. If you're excited, they'll become excited. Most groups end up reflecting the leader's values and attitudes. Consequently, with the Lord's help, you need to set a tempo that is friendly, positive, upbeat, inclusive, and caring.

The group's tempo or "climate" is important regardless of who is in the group, the group's purpose, or what the group does. It's best viewed as the human-relations foundation upon which your group or any group is built. Setting the tempo is both a crucial and an on-going resonsiblilty for a leader. I cannot overemphasize how important this step is to your group and your success as its leader.

I'll be honest with you, setting the group's pace isn't always an easy task. Many, many factors are at work. For example, the group's emotional and spiritual climate depends on the individual members themselves—their backgrounds, personalities, and prior experience in groups. These factors offer endless combinations and challenges. Nevertheless, you must account for these variations and their effect on the group's pace. Doing so is a vital, continuing responsibility. I'll say more about this topic later.

Provide structure— Among the tour guide's primary tasks is to plan and structure the trip. Can you imagine going on a trip with a guide who has neglected to make necessary arrangements and has no idea what to do? Likewise, your group members expect you to help them by providing logical order and direction for the group to get started, function, and accomplish its purpose.

Both philosophical and practical considerations are included in structuring your group. Why the group meets, when the group meets, where it meets, how long it meets, what the group does when it meets, individual members' responsibilities, and so on, are all initial issues needing organization. Usually the leader sets the pace by identifying these issues and suggesting possible alternatives. In some cases he or she determines these details without assistance, but this isn't recommended. A group needs to "own" its organizational structure. *How to Build a Small Groups Ministry* provides useful information for you and the group members on how to structure your group.

Providing initial structure is among your most important tasks. However, you also need to realize the group has the right to alter or completely change the preliminary structures you provide or suggest (but not always— some churches and organizations dictate how their groups must be structured and operate). As the leader, it's your responsibility to nurture the structuring process, not make all the decisions for the group. My next point deals with this idea.

Nurture key processes— Key among your general responsibilities is the obligation to facilitate two pivotal group processes: decision making and communication. A tour guide needs to assist fellow travelers in getting to know and relate to one another. Establishing good communication patterns is critical. Helping them make various decisions related to their journey also is expected. View yourself as being the group's decision-making and communications consultant.

Some key decision-making issues related to group structure were cited as we looked at your responsibility to provide structure. In addition, decision making is a fundamental process in dealing with conflicts in the group, evaluating the group's progress, adding new members, and a whole host of other things. Decision making, in fact, is the basic process underlying the group's day-to-day existence. A leader needs to develop skill at helping the group move through the decision-making process.

One final thought about group decision-making processes before moving on: It's important for you to understand that just because you are the leader, you are *not* responsible for making all the group's decisions. The group as a whole must accept accountability for determining its needs and actions. Occasionally, I encounter a group leader who has a warped perspective, for whatever reason, and thinks he or she ought to make all the group's decisions. This shouldn't happen. It reflects a leader who doesn't understand his or her role. Nurture and guide the process without making all the decisions or doing what the group should do for itself.

While decision making is an elemental process within a group, another process is even more central. It's a dynamic that you as the leader are expected to facilitate—namely, communication among the group members. Like all human endeavors, groups are dependent on good interpersonal communication. It's safe to say that healthy, open, honest, and frequent communication within the group is paramount to any group's success.

Volumes are written on group communication, so I won't say much more at this time. However, I do want to point out that the intricacies associated with human communication will provide some stretching experiences for you. Communication issues are among the most demanding of your time, skill, and patience as the group's leader. Here again, a key to success in this area is what you model. If you work at being a good communicator, your group usually follows suit.

One of the most critical processes you need to facilitate—one that includes both decision making and group communication—occurs early in the group's existence when the group establishes its covenant (see *How to Build a Small Groups Ministry* for more information on this topic). The covenanting process is arguably the most critical process and structuring tool affecting the group's overall success. Early in the group's life it establishes how it will function from that point on. Stay alert; you as leader are the key to this pivotal process.

Point out the sights along the way—"Now on your right is . . ." "Next, we'll stop to see . . ." "Over here is our . . ." Sound familiar? Every tour guide points out the sights during the trip; it's part of the job. Likewise, as a group leader you need to make certain you call your group members' attention to various dynamics taking place in the group's development and existence. This is one of the fun responsibilities you have as a group leader. I point out these dynamics, both good and not so good, throughout this book. You, in turn, need to make them known to your group.

I've quickly cited some general duties. Your situation likely involves each one, but as a group leader you need a specific job description, one that enumerates your exact role and responsibilities. It provides boundaries to guide your leadership role. A tour guide needs to know what's expected of him or her. If you weren't given a job description, write your own. In addition to defining your tasks, this vital document serves as a tool to help you evaluate your progress as a leader. If you find you have to develop your own, you might want to check out *How to Build a Small Groups Ministry* (see Recommended Resource List).

BUT CAN I SERVE AS THE GROUP'S GUIDE (LEADER)?

Is this your first time as a small group leader, a tour guide? Don't worry, every tour guide has to lead his or her *first* tour. Being a small group leader is no different. It's impossible for every leader to have extensive related experience before they lead a group. It doesn't work that way. In fact, most group leaders I talk with are leading their first group. You have to start somewhere and sometime. So, whether you're just beginning or are a highly experienced group leader, this section is important.

Our idealism about group leaders can propel us subconsciously into a fantasy excursion. Off we go on an idealized journey that lacks any reality. We find ourselves assuming that the leader must possess personal characteristics and abilities akin to God Himself. Our expectations for group leaders—ourselves or others—inflate to unrealistic levels. No wonder a lot of people are reluctant to become group leaders. But it needn't be this way.

Every book on small group leadership deals with group leadership skills. My three earlier books in this series are no exception; each considers the leader's personal traits or abilities to some degree. But this is good! In my opinion, the most important key to a small group's success is its leader. Don't let this scare you off. In fact, here are eight generalizations about serving as a group leader that provide both a realistic and an encouraging perspective.

1. Group leadership doesn't require a specific gender, temperament, or intelligence level. Having a male leader is only important if your theology or agenda dictates a "men only" position, as is the case with some church groups. Otherwise, women are just as good as men at leading groups. If the truth be known, I believe women often make better group leaders. They seem to have better instincts about people and groups than most men.

Sure, it helps to be an extrovert but this trait isn't *required.* People with average intelligence, even those who are quiet by nature, can make fine group leaders. I and a few of my colleagues joke that even engineers—who are notoriously non-relational (please forgive me if you're an engineer who doesn't fit this gross stereotype)—can become competent small group leaders.

2. Group leadership requires specific skills and abilities. In my thinking, group leadership is defined more by the skills and abilities associated with leading than by the leader's traits or characteristics. This book discusses many, but not all, of the skills and abilities associated with leading a small group.

3. Group leadership skills can be learned. Leading a group isn't like brain surgery. You and most people can master the skills necessary to do a fine job. Of course, you have to want to acquire and ultimately master the knowledge and behaviors needed to lead a group. The context or source for learning these facts and skills varies—on-the-job training, observation, reading, seminars, trial and error, and so forth—but guided experience is always the best teacher. Hook up with a skilled tour guide and pay attention to how he or she leads. Nothing is a better teacher than experience, especially experience critiqued by someone who can help you learn from your successes and failures.

4. Group leadership demands desire plus time and effort. Do you want to become a capable small group leader? Your desire to do so is perhaps the most important factor affecting your potential success. Positive personal motivation is indispensable. Next, your desire must be demonstrated by investing the time and effort needed to acquire the knowledge, skills, and experience associated with being a good group leader. Good leaders are made more frequently than they are born. It doesn't just happen. There aren't any shortcuts. Desire, time, and focused effort are all necessary.

5. Group leadership is shared. This is an important group characteristic. As I mentioned earlier when we talked about the group's dependence on you, a group should ultimately develop to a point where the majority of the group's functional leadership tasks are shared among all the members. This doesn't relieve you of all your leadership duties, but it does mean the group assumes the responsibility for most operational tasks associated with monitoring and caring for itself. In effect, the goal is for all members to become co-leaders.

Like the knowledge and skill you acquire as a leader, shared leadership must be learned and practiced. It is a group dynamic and goal that requires care and feeding. This is where you as the leader come in. Your responsibility is to introduce, explain, and help the group reach this desirable, mature stage in its development. Consult *How to Lead Small Groups* for more specifics on shared leadership.

6. Group leadership is situational. Different groups need different leadership. Some groups demand a great deal from their leader, others require very little. As a result, some leaders are very successful leading one type of group but find it difficult or impos-sible to lead some other kind of group. For example, I do much better leading task-oriented groups than I do leading growth groups or support groups. My left-brain orientation tends to dominate, and I frequently don't read people's emotional states very well.

Ideally, your group leadership skills will progress to a point where you can discern the kind or level of leadership a group needs and make whatever adjustments are called for providing what's needed. Some people call this "situational" leadership—you discern the situation and adjust as necessary. You are able to provide highly directive leadership for groups needing a forceful leader, non-directive leadership for groups that can act independently, or any leadership style in between. Having this ability to flex characterizes a master group leader. It's an art. Speaking of art, read the next point.

7. Group leadership is both an art and a science. You can learn everything there is to know about leading small groups but still not succeed in the task. Conversely, you may possess little or no information on how groups work but still be an outstanding small group leader. Neither extreme, however, is desirable. A balanced approach recognizes small group leadership as both an art and a science; you need both knowledge and an artistic touch.

While acknowledging that there is a science to leading groups — knowledge is critical — effective leaders more often than not are successful because they have a "feel" for leading groups. Their decisions and actions emerge from an internal process the leader cultivates through experience. They often develop a sixth sense whereby they are able to "read" the situation and respond accordingly. Such leaders are like skilled tour guides who know their territory so well that they rarely get lost and could almost lead blindfolded. Yet, even if you don't fit this category (I don't claim to) and never become a group "artist," you still can succeed at leading a group.

8. Group leadership is ministry. This is the most important idea for you to grasp about serving as a small group leader: Group leadership is a ministry. Burn this reality into your thinking. All of the skills, abilities, and methods we discuss in this book are only tools for you to use in ministering to your group members. Serving God by serving your group is a high calling you mustn't take for granted. Keeping a clear ministry focus is very helpful in battling the frustration and discouragement you'll encounter. Moreover, a strong ministry orientation takes away the temptation to center the group around you and your personality. After all, it is God's group, not yours — He is the real leader, you serve as His assistant. Be faithful in serving!

I want to wrap up this section on being a good tour guide by briefly sharing with you some ideas about group leadership, which come from research on the topic. In *Group Dynamics: The Psychology of Small Group Behavior* Marvin Shaw provides intriguing hypotheses on group leaders, formulated from his review of the literature. Let me summarize for you in my own words his six most relevant hypotheses.

Hypothesis 1 — Possessing task-related abilities and skills enhances your chance of attaining a leadership position.

This makes sense. If you already possess skills and abilities the group needs, it's more likely you will be given a leadership role.

Likewise, possessing such capabilities may cause you to seek a leadership position.

Hypothesis 2—Emergent leaders tend to be more authoritarian than leaders who are elected or appointed.

Persons who rise to group leadership roles in groups without a designated leader frequently do so because they possess strong personalities. They perhaps believe or discover they must behave autocratically in order to continue their position in the group, or such behavior may result from their strong motivation and self-oriented needs.

Hypothesis 3—Effective group leaders possess task-related abilities, are sociable, and are motivated to serve as the leader.

Successful leaders need to have knowledge and skills associated with the group's task. Sociability—applied interpersonal skills—is required to deal effectively with group members and the inevitable conflicts that occur. Moreover, a person must *want* to serve as the leader or at least agree to serve because he or she feels strongly about the group achieving its goals.

Hypothesis 4—Stressful situations tend to cause democratic leaders to behave in a more authoritarian manner.

As you can imagine, groups are more successful under democratic leadership. However, stressful situations within the group often cause the leader to adopt a more authoritarian leadership style. So, keep an eye on yourself when dealing with stressful situations in your group.

Hypothesis 5—The leader's source of authority influences both the leader's behavior and the group members' reactions.

Sometimes group leaders are pastors, other church leaders, or "powerful" persons within the community or church. It's common for such leaders to act accordingly. Consequently, they are viewed by the group members as being different from themselves, causing them to treat the leader in a deferential manner.

Hypothesis 6 — The degree to which the leader is accepted by the other group members depends on whether or not the group is achieving its goals.

The group's success is the leader's success and vice versa. If the group is struggling, often its difficulties are projected onto the leader. Helping the group achieve its reason for existing is usually viewed as a result of your positive leadership.

I found these hypotheses interesting. Did you? Which ones do you think are relevant or apply to your current situation? After considering these questions, read on.

KNOW WHERE YOU'RE GOING

Can you imagine going on a trip with a tour guide who has no idea where he or she is going, but is eager to take you there? As improbable as this sounds, it isn't all that uncommon among small groups. Many leaders are excited about leading a group, yet have no particular destination in mind. Consequently their groups travel aimlessly about, accomplishing little, and tiring prematurely.

Knowing where you're going is best determined by identifying two basic features: (1) the kind or type of group and (2) its related purpose or goals. Nailing down these two issues puts you in the driver's seat. Success isn't guaranteed, but at least your chances are greatly increased.

I review group types in chapter 10 of this book. *How to Build a Small Groups Ministry* (see Recommended Resource List) also discusses different kinds of groups and information on determining your group's purpose and goals. There is no one way or right way to do groups. The options are endless. Just make certain you know where you're going on your journey.

Determining your group's direction may or may not be your decision. Most frequently it's not totally up to you. Still, it's likely you *are* responsible for the decision-making process to determine the group's destination. To pull it off, you need to familiarize yourself with the options and be prepared to help your group sort through the possibilities.

Frequently, a group's destination is determined prior to launching out, but not always. In a few cases the members get together and then decide what kind of group they want and what they hope to accomplish. This strategy is usually employed by groups whose members are experienced with small groups and want to continue their involvement. The group's type and purpose are important but are secondary to maintaining the experience itself. Groups, good groups, can become a way of life.

Here's a twist: the tour company may already have set the itinerary. It's common for people to sign up for prearranged tour packages. My brother and sister-in-law enjoy going on cruises where everything is predetermined; they just go along. A similar dynamic is often true in many, if not most, church small group programs. The church develops specific groups for specific purposes and then invites its members and other interested people to come along. Group participants may participate in determining a few administrative details— such as time and place—but don't have input on the group's purpose or the goals. Fellowship groups and Bible studies are two types of groups that commonly fall into this category.

Determining where you're going is absolutely mandatory. But your destination may change. It's conceivable that your group or your church leadership may decide to do things differently or change courses altogether. The logic for doing so may be obvious or just a response to a "feel" the group gets. Either way, hopefully all the pros and cons are clearly identified before the group switches gears.

YOU'LL GET LOST A TIME OR TWO

Let me forewarn you: it's almost certain you'll get lost at least a few times during your journey as a group. It's normal. Don't fret. Getting lost—not knowing what to do, encountering a situation you cannot handle, facing a difficult relationship, discovering hidden agendas— is a normal occurrence in every group. I've never participated in a perfect group, a group that didn't face a problem or two along the way.

The real question isn't *if* your group will lose its way, but how you will react *when* it happens. My advice is simple: don't panic; keep moving. Your role as leader makes you the person responsible, especially in the group's early stages, to help the group find its way and get back on track. You may spin your wheels a bit, but that's okay. Eventually, with God's help and your focused effort, you'll succeed at getting back in the groove.

Getting confused, sidetracked, or "lost" isn't soley a group issue. The group may be just fine—you personally may encounter a confusing situation, brought on by the group or your own personal or spiritual life. If this occurs, just remember God is on your side and can provide the strength to weather whatever storm you are battling. Furthermore, don't forget you also are a group member. Turning to your fellow group members for help models an attitude and behavior you hope they will emulate. You're not an island; you aren't expected to go it on your own.

In chapter 4, "We're Off," we'll deal with some specific challenges you'll encounter in guiding your group. But for now, let me suggest a three-pronged strategy to utilize when you find the group or yourself "lost."

1. Prayer—Prayer is the group leader's most valuable tool. Stay plugged in to the power source. If you want to succeed, you will do so only if your group ministry is saturated in prayer. First Thessalonians 5:17 exhorts us to "pray without ceasing." Pray for wisdom, insight, your group members, and the following two characteristics.

2. Persistence—Keep on keeping on. Don't give up at the first sign of trouble or disappointment. Drive on! Sure there will be times when you want to chuck it all. Resist the urge! God will give you perseverance if you ask. Remember, God may choose to bring tribulations to build your perseverance and prove your character (see Romans 5:3-4). Being a group leader, and the Christian life in general, requires persistence.

3. Patience—Group leadership also demands patience. If you're like me, this divine characteristic is difficult to practice. God is patient with me, but I have real trouble being patient with others (just ask my wife). Yet, 1 Thessalonians 5:14 requires us to be patient with everyone. Likewise, 2 Timothy 2:24 asks us to be patient when wronged. Thankfully, being patient is another skill God teaches if you ask.

TAKING ACTION

1. Describe your feelings about serving as your group's "tour guide."

2. Thinking about the tour guide's general responsibilities (pp. 18-23), which is an area of strength and which makes you the most nervous? What can you do to overcome your nervousness?

3. Review the six hypotheses on group leadership (pp. 26-28) and select the one that applies to you most. Explain your selection.

4. Describe what kind or type of group you are leading and list your goals (what you hope to accomplish).

5. Knowing prayer, persistence, and patience are needed, identify anything else you think you need to succeed as a small group "tour guide."

CHAPTER THREE

Pre-Trip Preparation

*Put GOD in charge of your work,
then what you've planned will take place.*
Proverbs 16:3, *The Message*

E VERY trip begins before you leave. My family's anticipation
began building many months prior to our actual departure.
Going to Israel took preparation. Our expectations were escalating;
we wanted to know about our itinerary, who we were going with,
what our fellow travelers were like, and what we must take with
us. We couldn't leave yet—we needed time to prepare. Our anticipation kept us motivated right up until the time we departed.
Important issues needed to be addressed if we were going to have
an excellent trip.

My family's pre-trip experience parallels what most groups
encounter. There are issues to consider prior to actually beginning a
group, and your group is no exception. Investing time to finalize
pre-trip preparations is smart. Doing so greatly increases the likelihood your group will develop into a real, functional group.

This chapter explores various preliminary steps necessary to
build a solid future for your group. All the issues we discuss are
essential and must be attended to, ideally, prior to your group's
first meeting. This doesn't mean you cannot or will not change one
or more expectations at some point, but these issues need attention
now, before you start out. You are laying the foundation for your
group's success.

TOUR EXPECTATIONS

We hadn't even left yet, but in talking with friends who had already been to Israel, my family and I began developing expectations for our own trip. Our minds were filled with anticipation. We constantly thought about how neat the trip would be and what we wanted to see and do. The closer the time came to embark, the more excited we became.

Just as we anticipated our trip, it's normal for you and your members or potential members to have expectations about being in a group. Every human endeavor we take part in causes us to develop certain expectations. Small groups are no different.

As the leader, you have various expectations—for yourself, for individual members, and for the group as a whole. A wise leader identifies and sorts through these expectations in order to prepare for the journey. Doing so potentially avoids numerous difficulties that may arise. Here are some typical expectations you and other leaders may have.

- I can do this, with God's help.
- I want to do a good job.
- The members need to take being in the group seriously.
- I want the members to appreciate my efforts.
- The members need to help me make the group a success.

Group members also have expectations—for themselves, for you as their leader, and for the group as a whole. Often these are conscious expectations they openly express. But it's also likely they have hidden expectations they are reluctant to talk about or unconscious expectations they aren't aware of, which pop up later during the group's journey. The members' expressed or hidden expectations (personal, interpersonal, group, administrative, and so on) are far too numerous to list, but here is a small sample.

- We cannot allow Sarah to dominate the group.
- I don't want the leader to make me pray out loud.
- The group needs to finish on time.
- I need the leader to acknowledge my participation.
- We need to spend more time praying together.

- I want the group members to like me.
- The group must meet on a weekly basis.

You'll find yourself dealing with group expectations at various times in a group's existence—before the group begins, early in the group's development, as the group matures, and finally as the group comes to its end. Expectations can and do change. People aren't static. It's common for us to change our minds, develop new needs, see things differently, or respond to unexpected crises in our lives. When this happens, it is normal for our desires and expectations to shift. Therefore, I bring up this topic again at various times throughout this book.

Truth in advertising is absolutely necessary. Building false expectations isn't acceptable. In fact, it is unethical. You wouldn't want to go on a trip and find out everything the travel company told you was bogus. Similarly, be up front and honest about your group— its purpose, goals, organizational structure, and relationships, for example. Make sure you don't promise more than you can or hope to deliver. It's okay to speculate on all the benefits you hope to realize in the group, but a conservative estimate presented in tentative terms is your best approach.

You cannot please everyone. On our trip to Israel one nice couple objected a lot. Their expectations weren't being met. They assumed the tour's pace was going to be much slower than it turned out to be. Sound familiar? You can expect something similar in your group. It is a rare event when a group is able to meet everyone's expectations. I mention this because some rookie leaders mistakenly think their role is to make everyone happy. Sure, this is a worthy leadership goal to pursue, but don't become distressed when it doesn't happen.

So, as the group's leader, how do you go about determining and dealing with pre-trip expectations? An answer to this question is possible from two different perspectives. The first option occurs when you already know who is in your group, and they are helping you plan how the group will function. In this case your method is fairly straightforward—just budget time to talk about what you and the others expect from being in a group together. As the leader, you take the lead in this pivotal discussion. Share your own expectations first, then allow the other members to share theirs. The goal is to formulate a mutual set of expectations everyone can buy into. Yet don't be disheartened if one or two persons decide to withdraw when they discover their needs and desires don't match with the other members'. Thank them for their participation up to that point, and encourage them to find another group more suitable to their needs.

A second option is to deal with the members' initial expectations during the group's first few meetings. This strategy is required when the members aren't involved in pre-group planning, when they just show up and want to join the group. This situation is the most common. In chapter 4, I outline how to deal with expectations in this context.

If you permit new members to join the group after it has been functioning for a while, don't forget to make certain they understand the group's purpose, your goals, and the group's expectations they must observe as members. In addition, you're smart to give them the opportunity to express any expectations they have for being in the group. After all, they now influence the group. Their wants, desires, and opinions will affect how the group operates and will contribute to or detract from the group's success. In effect, your group is starting all over again.

Adding new members to an existing group causes upheaval in the group's relationships and functioning. Nevertheless, some people advocate this option. I don't, especially for certain types of groups. My reasons for thinking this way are covered in both *How to Lead Small Groups* and *How to Build a Small Groups Ministry* (see Recommended Resource List).

Dealing with expectations is your job. Failure to do so almost certainly will cause problems somewhere down the line. And since expectations can change at various points in the group's existence, it is wise for you to understand a group's developmental stages. Review the chart on the next page, adapted from *How to Lead Small Groups*. My aim is to alert you briefly to the basic issues you can expect during the group's journey.

Having a good grasp of a group's life cycle can serve you well. After all, you're also allowed to have expectations. Surely you hope to achieve certain things. It's normal. Leading a group and achieving your expectations is greatly enhanced if you know and understand the stages a group goes through in becoming a real group. Consequently, in future chapters I note specific group developmental issues related to the various group life cycles.

THE SMALL GROUP LIFE CYCLE

Because you as the leader intend to help your small group become a fully functioning group, it is vital to understand the phases or stages a group goes through during its lifetime. Group development closely follows the various phases of human development—from conception through adulthood and old age. This makes sense because people make up groups. The following *generalizations* assume the group meets weekly for one year.

Phase One—*Birth and Infancy (Forming; 2-3 sessions)* A group's life cycle begins even before the group first meets. Once the group begins meeting, it is vital to clarify purpose, structure, relationships, and expectations. During this phase most members are very dependent on the leader. Consequently, the leader must set the pace and demonstrate high initiative.

Phase Two—*Childhood (Norming; 6-7 sessions)* A time for testing—the members are learning what is and isn't acceptable as group members. Focus is on establishing boundaries or norms to govern the group. Any initial conflict is resolved and members' participation is affirmed. Individualism is giving way to group identity and function.

Phase Three—*Teenager (Conforming; 5-6 sessions)* Questioning and adjustment occur during this third phase. Members begin to challenge group norms and practices, personal and group modifications are considered, and the group struggles with the need to accept responsibility for itself. Once the group has resolved its teenage issues it is ready to begin functioning as a mature group.

Phase Four—*Maturity (Performing; 30 sessions)* The individuals are now a group. Hopefully the longest phase, the group's purpose and goals are now being realized. Shared leadership is emerging and helping the group maintain its relationships, procedures, and details. Holding off boredom and ineffectiveness is required. Some evaluation and adjustments are needed.

Phase Five—*Old Age and Demise (Reforming; 5-6 sessions)* The group has been together now for nearly a year and is nearing its conclusion. Ending the group on a positive note and paving the way for the members' future involvement in groups is paramount. Celebrating struggles and successes is vital, as is dealing with the "grief process" effective groups may experience. The group may elect to re-covenant and continue on.

PLANNING THE ITINERARY

Successful tours have well-thought-out itineraries. Travel agencies are willing to plan your trip down to the last detail—airline tickets, accommodations, daily schedule, ground transportation, tickets to entertainment events, and so on. After all, it's their business to help you. They want you to have a good time.

Some churches act like travel agencies. An oversight committee plans all the details associated with small groups sponsored by that church. All you need to do is show up and have a good time. There is nothing left for you to do other than attend the meetings on a regular basis. Sometimes this approach works. Some group members prefer having everything prearranged. It takes the guesswork out of being in a group and even helps them decide if they want join a group in the first place.

Some people like to plan their own trip. Like a family planning its summer vacation, group members sit down and determine what kind of group they want and specify goals they hope to achieve. In their opinion, "It's our trip and we want to plan it ourselves." Groups in this category are responsible for themselves, and few or no expectations are placed on them by their churches (organizations, sponsors, and so on). They are free to select the structural and functional details they wish.

Whether the group is preplanned by someone else or the group itself makes its plans, you as the leader still play an important role. You might serve on an oversight committee to plan a groups ministry involving many groups, formulate by yourself the structure for one group, or join the decision-making process among group members who are planning their group. In any case you play a critical part in helping to determine the group's appropriate structure and organizational details. We briefly discussed these structural and organizational issues back in chapter 2. Ensuring that these items are attended to allows the members to invest their energies in becoming a real group. More material on preplanning can be found in *How to Build a Small Groups Ministry* and *How to Have Great Small Groups* (see Recommended Resource List).

WHO'S GOING WITH YOU?

"Everybody is welcome!" proclaims the travel brochure. But sometimes this isn't true. There are special trips planned for certain destinations, select individuals, or specific groups. Every trip I've been on seemed to appeal to certain people whose age, background, or interests were in keeping with the trip's destination and itinerary. Small groups often follow this same pattern. The group's purpose and goals dictate who should participate — anyone who is willing or people who fit into a designated category.

Among the most important issues you must resolve prior to starting your group is the basic question: *Who is eligible to join this group?* The question is more difficult to answer than it first appears. Some folks balk at the word "eligible." It goes against their grain. They prefer to champion a "y'all come" approach rather than putting restrictions on who can or cannot join. This open invitation works for some groups, but not necessarily for *all* groups.

Criteria for group membership is a topic I include in all my books on small groups. Why? Because after leadership, it's the most important factor influencing the group's success. Who is in your group makes a big difference as to whether or not the members gel as a group and accomplish the group's purpose for existence. Yet, realistically speaking, in most cases it is unlikely you can have total control over who is or isn't in your group.

I wish it were true that everyone got along with everyone else and had similar needs and interests. Nice idea, but it just doesn't work that way. The obvious truth is that people are different. And while the body of Christ is diverse, inclusive, and multidimensional, our "old sin nature" prevents us from functional unity and harmony. In some groups it's worth trying to overcome our differences, to invite anyone and everyone to join. Other groups are much more effective if they serve a specific category of people. How do you sort out what to do? There is no one, fixed easy answer.

Allow me to share my experience with you by stating seven practical guidelines I follow.

1. Birds of a feather flock together. This first principle is common knowledge. People tend to feel most comfortable with other people like themselves. "Like themselves" may include obvious things like age, education, social status, religion, ethnicity, gender, or unique characteristics such as denominational identity, a shared crisis, occupation, or particular interest. When given the option, most people tend to participate in groups, or anything else, in which they feel comfortable. They don't want to stick out or feel different. You may not like this tendency, but it's a reality. Churches, schools, social clubs, and entertainment all reflect this facet of human nature.

2. You cannot force people. No matter what I think is the best way to group people, attempts to "force" (compel, coerce, pressure) them into a particular group rarely works. We live in a society where individual freedom reigns supreme. People, even Christians, resist being told what to do and how to do it. I've seen people drive all the way across town because they prefer to participate in a particular group, for whatever reasons, rather than attend a group in their own neighborhood.

3. Some groups attract a certain membership. I'm not going to attend a support group for people with a gambling addiction because I don't have a problem with this issue. I'm not likely to attend a women's Bible study. Likewise, I may or may not participate in a task-oriented group convened to plan and oversee my church's youth ministry. You get the point: some groups by their very nature dictate who is eligible to attend.

4. Age-graded groups work best. In general, groups formulated around the members' age seem to work better than other options. People the same age, give or take about ten years, have many things in common — family ages, social practices, cultural norms, economic issues, and so on. Conversely, groups that attempt to include younger adults with older adults frequently experience difficulty. Such groups can work, but they demand extra time and effort on the leader's part. This is also true for groups that attempt to include children on a regular basis (an option I don't recommend; the maturity gap between children and adults is too wide, resulting in a group that meets neither age group's needs).

5. Some things don't matter. Apart from issues related to age, other things usually don't seem to matter when it comes to group membership. Generally speaking, I've found factors such as rich or poor, men or women, black or white, educated or uneducated aren't issues that prevent a group from succeeding. Apparently limited diversity doesn't hinder group development and may even promote understanding among people the same age. In groups sponsored by churches, personal or cultural diversity usually isn't a big issue anyway. Most churches tend to serve a narrowly defined social and cultural group, for example, white middle-class churches, African-American urban churches, rural farming churches, or upper-class mainline churches. I'm not arguing that this is the way it should be; I'm merely pointing out the way it is.

6. Alternatives are necessary. Not everyone wants to go to the same place with the same people. Put in other words, it is important to offer more than one kind of group, held at different times, and with various purposes. This fact may or may not affect the one group you lead, but it must definitely be included in a church's thinking when planning a small groups ministry.

7. Choice works best. The six previous guidelines lead to this last obvious conclusion: Whenever possible, I prefer to give people a choice, to let them choose which group they want. In the end, most people go where they want to go anyway, or don't go at all. You have to decide whether it's important to have them in the "right" group, some group, or no group.

Okay, I hear your protests. Yes, I agree with you. Ideally the body of Christ shouldn't make distinctions between people. Personal factors such as age, gender, education, or race should not play a part in formulating group membership. Christians should be able to participate in any group with anyone. I've read Acts 15:9, Romans 3:22 and 10:12, and Ephesians 4:4. But these passages speak about membership within the body, not Christians functioning in small groups. As difficult as it may be, when it comes to groups you need to decide who is eligible to be in your specific group. If you elect "y'all come," which is a perfectly acceptable option, be prepared to deal with the diversity and struggles you'll face in attempting to get the members to become a real group.

KNOW YOUR TRAVEL PARTNERS

You cannot be certain what a person is really like until you spend time with him or her. On our family trip we became good friends with several families. Spending time together—sharing the journey—

brought us closer together and deepened our relationships. This same dynamic also is true for your group members. Relationships make the group a group. Strong relationships are the glue that binds the members together.

Groups are a collection of individuals who move from an "I," "me," "my" identity to a "we," "us," "our" focus. This change in focus and adoption of a group identity requires you to establish personal relationships with your fellow group members. Three different contexts facilitate this basic expectation.

1. One-on-one. The truth be known, you cannot have a relationship with a group — with the people in the group, yes; with the group itself, no. One-on-one interaction is the group's most basic relational building block. As leader, the time you spend getting to know each member as an individual is perhaps the most constructive time you invest in helping the group. Likewise, all the group members need to build one-on-one relationships with you and each other.

2. Within the group. Relationship building also must happen within the group itself. During the group meetings, especially in the beginning, it is important to budget time for the members to introduce themselves, share their "story," and become comfortable with one another. Make certain you don't neglect to include this activity so essential to group development. In fact, you may find it necessary to invest two or three early group meetings to well-planned relationship building, depending on the type of group you are leading.

3. Outside the group. Effective groups invariably achieve this status because the members spend time together outside the regular group meetings. It's not a requirement; they want to spend time together. Relationships progress to a point where members aren't satisfied limiting themselves to the short time they are together during group meetings. Members actively plan or just find opportunities to spend more time with each other. While all or just a few members may participate, I've noticed that really successful groups tend to have a majority of their members involved in these additional informal activities.

Getting to know your group members in any context may happen by chance, or you can take deliberate steps to make sure it happens. I'll wager you know what I'm going to recommend. Once your group members are "signed up," invest time getting to know them and assist them in getting to know each other. Much of what we talk about from this point forward is intended to promote and nurture this critical, underlying process.

In the next chapter we will examine a few ideas on how you can help your group during its first few meetings to get to know and appreciate each other. But for now, I'd like to suggest several things most group members like to know, or need to know, about each other:

- Name
- If married, how long, how they met their spouse
- Family particulars: children, grandchildren, and so on
- Occupation
- Unique accomplishments, personal abilities, interests
- Church background
- Personal spiritual journey
- Prior group experience and expected gains from this group

A PRE-TRIP CHECKLIST

A checklist often is provided by travel agencies to help you make certain you are prepared for the trip. It's a good idea. Having briefly covered various factors involved in pre-trip planning, the things you need to nail down prior to the group's first meeting, and variables that build a foundation necessary for your group to develop into a real group, the following checklist provides you with an opportunity to make certain everything is in order prior to heading out.

- The group's purpose and goals are identified (or you're prepared to lead the group in a decision-making process to identify these and the other issues listed below).
- You have a good understanding of your own expectations.
- The group's "itinerary" is planned (this big issue is considered only briefly in this chapter).
- You understand the stages a group goes through during its lifetime.
- Group membership eligibility is determined.
- A plan is developed to facilitate relationship building among the members.

STAY ON THE ROAD AND KEEP GOING

Once the trip is started, you need to stay on the road and keep going. Leave the trail, and you're likely to get lost. I remember one lady with us on our trip to Israel who decided to turn left to look in a shop while all the rest of us went straight ahead to the next site our guide wanted us to see. Several minutes later when we arrived at our destination, her husband noticed she wasn't with the group. Panic set in. The whole tour plan was derailed while we developed an alternative plan and sent people out looking for the missing tourist. Fortunately, we finally found her and were able to resume our sightseeing.

Once your group begins, make certain you stay on track and stick with your plan. You'll be tempted to stray away when trouble erupts, a new idea strikes, or a member suggests an enticing alternative. Resist! Be forewarned: Deviating from your well-designed plan greatly increases the difficulty the group faces in its ability to gel and become a "real" group. Constantly changing directions gets people lost. Besides, relationships are the most important dynamic you need to establish early on. I find once these group relationships are secured, or at least well on their way, any needed organizational or administrative adjustments come much easier.

The time may come when you need or want to make some adjustments, but during the first months the group meets, focus on your initial plan and on establishing relationships. It is difficult to make informed decisions about potential changes if you haven't yet established an operational pattern. Moreover, you'll discover the members become restless if you don't get into a productive "groove" and maintain some stability. No one likes to participate in a group that is in constant flux or in which they don't sense they are building strong relationships.

Remind yourself: *I can do this!* Sure, you're likely to experience one or two challenges, but you're also destined to benefit greatly from your commitment and hard work. God has good things in store for you! Satan doesn't want you to succeed, but don't worry: " . . . *the Lord is faithful, and He will strengthen and protect you from the evil one*" (2 Thessalonians 3:3).

To finish off this chapter and prepare you for launching out on your impending group journey, here are some random pieces of final advice I'd like to share with you.

- Depend on the Holy Spirit.
- Relax, be yourself and have fun.
- Your leadership role is important, but don't take yourself too seriously.
- Practice flexibility.
- Admit your mistakes.
- Make the group members feel comfortable.
- Be a good listener.
- Always be prepared.
- Know whom to ask for help.
- Invest the amount of time needed.
- Help the members practice shared leadership.
- Remember, leading a small group is a ministry.

In the next chapter we focus on starting your group off on the right foot, which increases your groups chances of becoming a real group.

TAKING ACTION

1. Describe any expectations you or your group members have for being in a group together.

2. Understanding the group's life cycle is important (see chart, p. 37). Is there any phase you don't understand? If yes, determine what you can do to gain a better understanding.

3. Who is "eligible" to join your group and how did you make this determination?

4. Outline a plan whereby you and the group members can get to know each other. Be sure to include options for all three contexts.

5. Are all the items listed on the Pre-Trip Checklist complete (pages 43-44)? If no, what do you still have to do prior to setting out on your small group journey?

6. A list of advice concludes the chapter. Which statement seemed to speak to you the most?

CHAPTER FOUR

We're Off

The ways of right-living people glow with light;
the longer they live, the brighter they shine.
Proverbs 4:18, *The Message*

BEGINNING a journey is exciting. Anticipation is high, energy is flowing, people are enthusiastic. Capturing and channeling this momentum becomes a significant task for the leader. It is your prime opportunity to establish the group's tone, direction, and relationships.

This chapter explores issues related to the first two stages in a group's life cycle or development, *birth and infancy* and *childhood*. The group is just beginning. Everything and, most likely, everyone are new. It's the opportune time to establish productive patterns. Virtually everything you do here at the start—both administratively and relationally—will come back to either promote or plague the group. Consequently, the first few meetings are crucially important and must not be taken for granted.

GETTING A GOOD START

Most groups are a bit "nervous" at first. The members are cautious, watchful, and waiting. A few might even be a little suspicious and doubtful. Having experienced group failures and disappointments in the past, they aren't getting their hopes up. In addition, some people may be attending for the wrong reasons. His wife made him come. She wants to please a member who is her boss at work. They hope to convince the members to adopt a specific doctrinal practice. These and many other questionable or positive motives are potentially in the mix. As the leader you are facing a big task, but with God's promised help you can succeed (Hebrews 4:16).

Fostering a good start is now your primary concern. All your energies must focus on planning and leading initial group meetings that achieve specific objectives related to group formation—especially relationship building. In addition to any content objectives you set for these initial meetings, here are seven group developmental (with emphasis on relational) objectives you need to accomplish within the first seven to ten sessions.

1. Establish yourself as the group's leader.
2. Ensure individual members are made to feel comfortable and welcome.
3. Give all the members an opportunity to fully introduce themselves.
4. Determine or explain the group's purpose and goals.
5. Define mutually acceptable group norms.
6. Review the general intent behind becoming a group, including Christian community.
7. Clarify group organizational and administrative details.

Pursuing these objectives starts with the very first meeting. The specific agenda depends on the type of group you're leading, but without exception it is wise to budget time for the members to introduce themselves and to review the group's purpose for meeting. I also recommend you establish ground rules (group norms) to govern how you operate as a group, but usually that comes a little later, around the third or fourth meeting. But in some groups, task-oriented groups for example, it is common to accomplish all these things at the first meeting. Most groups, however, require multiple meetings to work through the preliminaries. Furthermore, there is no one set format, agenda, or strategy every group must follow. Each group is different. Your group must proceed in its own way and on its own timetable.

Good news! Resources are available to help you plan your first meetings. Check the Recommended Resource List in the back of this book. These or other resources you may find at your Christian bookstore are practical guides designed to assist you in planning and conducting productive meetings from the very beginning. Moreover, they suggest methods that are appropriate to achieve all the group developmental dynamics we are talking about in this book—even though you may have to do a little tweaking to make such areas as methods, activities, and timing fit your specific group.

As you get started, in many cases you'll find the new group members are polite and withhold any criticism or complaints that may arise during the first or maybe second meetings. They don't feel comfortable yet and are hesitant to express strong opinions. Use this grace period to establish yourself and set the tone for your leadership. Grasp the opportunity to demonstrate your eagerness and excitement.

In addition, participants need to experience an early success—something they can feel good about, a positive outcome. Doing so reinforces their eager attitudes and instills a favorable outlook for the future. For instance, they need to find out you really care about them, they have characteristics or interests in common with the other members, you aren't expecting them to do anything weird (some people have strange ideas about what they might be asked to do in a small group), or perhaps something as simple as finishing the group meeting on time. I can't list all the options, but I know you understand what I am getting at.

As I've already said, your actions and attitudes set the tone and establish the group's early atmosphere. So, here are ten "rules of the game." Use these early in the group's existence (and keep using as long as the group meets) to help build their confidence and your credibility.

1. Explain your "credentials." Members are interested to know about your group background, if you've led a group before, what your goals are, and what they can expect from you. If you have limited experience, don't worry about it: tell the members. Explain that it isn't "your" group, but "our" group. Their involvement and ideas are just as important as your own. Your role is to guide the group, with their help, in becoming a real group.

2. Be enthusiastic and happy about doing your "thing." Show them you are excited about being in and leading the group.

3. Display self-confidence; it makes people feel "safe" and comfortable.

4. Believe in the group and remain optimistic about the group's probable success; it gives members confidence and encouragement.

5. Share your knowledge about groups so they know you can take them where they need to go. People want to feel the leader has things under control and everything will go smoothly. They want to believe group membership is an enriching experience.

6. Make the group confident about your ability to prevent disasters and handle difficult people and situations.

7. Demonstrate to the group that you are organized and know where you are going. At the same time, be sure they know you aren't rigid, manipulative, controlling, or inflexible.

8. Practice an active sense of humor. Members appreciate it if you don't take yourself too seriously. Everyone should have fun in the group.

9. Make sure the group knows that you hear them, and that you are responsive to their needs and concerns. Their trust in you is increased when they see you accept their ideas and opinions on group matters.

10. Be certain the group experiences early success so the members have hope and optimism about even greater success ahead.

FINDING YOUR SEAT

You arrive at the airport, check your baggage in, and after a short wait it's time to board the plane. Standing at the gate is a friendly employee, eager to assist you. At the other end of the boarding ramp another person waits at the plane's door, ready to help you find your seat.

This is the standard boarding routine of a commercial airline. Applying this concept to small groups, we are talking about helping each member find their "seat" in the group. Doing so is both figurative and literal.

Speaking figuratively, each member needs to sense he or she is welcome and fits into the group. Members must quickly discern how their participation is needed, that their opinions and ideas are welcome, that they have a stake in the group's processes, and that the group's future is dependent in part on their involvement. No one single activity, method, or word from you finalizes these seating issues. It is a process like walking down the plane's aisle. Every group member needs to find his or her figurative seat and sit down.

Helping the members find their seat also demands some literal, practical actions on your part. When the group members arrive for the very first meeting you need to:

1. Be there to set up before anyone arrives—make sure the furniture is comfortable and arranged in a "friendly" manner (so everyone can see everyone else), the lighting is adequate, and the temperature is comfortable. Doing these things is easy if the group meets in your home. If not, be diplomatic.

2. Greet each arrival at the front door—be cheerful and upbeat, express your pleasure at seeing them and having them in the group. I am talking about genuine friendliness, not some put-on act. Be yourself, but be at your best.

3. Escort them into the room where you meet and politely suggest where they might wish to sit. If possible, avoid having the first people sit in the "back" of the room (by the entry), thus making it difficult for subsequent people to quickly enter and find a seat. Also be sure people don't hide by sitting behind a lamp, in the next room, or in some other position that places them outside the group. But in the final analysis, let them sit where they want.

4. Continue the greeting process until everyone has arrived. As you bring new individuals into the room, make sure you briefly introduce them to those already there. Long introductions aren't necessary since more formal self-introductions come later.

Of course, these four steps only illustrate my general idea. Feel free to devise a routine that fits your personality and your specific group.

Future meetings may not require such focused effort, but you would be shrewd to never completely abandon greeting and welcoming your members when they arrive. Hopefully, as the group matures, your fellow group members will become more involved in this relational activity and the need for you to always be the "greeter" will diminish.

Do you serve refreshments as they arrive, at the end, or not at all? It's your call. There is no right answer. I personally think *simple* refreshments are a nice idea. If you do serve something, let me make these suggestions. First, keep it basic. Elaborate goodies aren't necessary and are not recommended. Second, make certain you don't waste time. It's easy to let the refreshments gobble up time better spent on the group meeting itself. This is especially true if you serve at the beginning. Finally, there is nothing wrong with the members drinking coffee or whatever during the meeting. Still, I wouldn't serve anything else until the meeting is finished.

BECOMING TRAVEL PARTNERS

Great trips result from good planning, attention to details, a fun itinerary, and most importantly, great traveling companions. I've traveled to some not so terrific places with some terrific people and had a superb time. On the other hand, going to a fantastic location wasn't much fun when I went with people who were grouchy and unfriendly. Your travel partners make a *big* difference.

In chapter 3 we discussed some basics issues related to who is in your group and about the need to get to know your travel partners. Now the process begins in earnest.

Once in a while everyone in your group is there because you "picked" them; they responded to your personal invitation to participate. Far more often the members come from various sources — they talked with a friend, the church office told them, they signed up on a list passed around in your Sunday school class, or a pastor recommended the group. I mention this because even though your travel partners make a big difference, rarely do you actually get to choose who goes on the journey with you. Consequently, it is of paramount importance that you invest adequate time in building a "partnership" among the group members. The group's success is at stake.

Becoming travel partners involves two relational elements. First, the members need to feel comfortable with you as their travel guide — their group leader — and with being in the group in general. This earliest segment starts, even before they attend the first meeting, with any initial contact you have with them, no matter how brief.

If you already know who is in your group or who specifically plans to attend the first meeting, I recommend you call them prior to the meeting just to say hello, to make sure they have the correct time and place, and to answer any questions they may have. Potential members usually are pleased by your early efforts to reach out to them.

This first relational element also is established by how you greet them when they *arrive* at the first meeting, as we described a few paragraphs ago. First impressions are *very* important. But you know that. How you treat them *during* the first few meetings is also critical. They need to sense that you have a genuine interest in them, that you like them, and that they are welcome to like you. You communicate these feelings and this information both by what you say and don't say. People read body language as well as hearing your words.

Members must also begin building relationships with the other members. Sometimes all the members already know each other and relationship building occurs rapidly. But most often a few individuals know each other, a few are somewhat acquainted, and several are strangers. The real trick is to balance out the group's relationship mix. You need to do something to facilitate an introduction process whereby everyone has the opportunity to get to know each other. This critical relationship "leveling" process establishes the group's relational atmosphere and lays the foundation for the group's upcoming decision-making processes.

I routinely invest the first two or maybe even three meetings doing introductions, especially when it is a relationship or need-oriented group. I'm not as concerned when it comes to content or task-oriented groups because such groups don't emphasize relationships as a prime reason for meeting. Nevertheless, regardless of its specific type, every group must spend time making certain its members know each other. It's not a waste of time. Even task-oriented groups function much better when the members know each other and spend a little time talking about what being a group means.

Where to start? I always begin the first meeting on time, thank them for coming, and then introduce myself. My introductory remarks include such things as my "name, rank, and serial number"; how pleased I am to have them in the group; what I see as the group's *potential* purpose and goals (I'm much more definite if the church or organization sponsoring the group has predetermined these issues); something about my background in groups and leading groups; what we will do together during the first few meetings; and the decisions, if any, the group needs to make about organizational and administrative details. Finally, I invite them to ask any questions they may have based on what I just said or about the group in general. Don't be surprised if your introduction, comments, and their questions consume the better part of the first meeting.

Please consider what I do as only one suggestion. You may choose, of course, to add or subtract items when you introduce yourself to your group. But I strongly recommend you start with your own introduction and not wait until last. How you go about introducing yourself usually sets the pattern everyone else follows. Besides, the extra time the members have to merely sit in the group and listen to you helps them relax and develop nonverbal association with you and the other members.

Next, after introducing myself, I ask the members to introduce themselves. If I already know someone well, I ask him or her to start the process. Otherwise I just ask the person on my right (or left, it doesn't matter) to begin and go around the room until everyone has had the opportunity to speak for himself or herself. In a humorous fashion, I ask married individuals not to introduce their spouses, other than to acknowledge who belongs to whom. In addition, I ask them to please include certain specific information in their introductions. You can ask your members to include anything you want, but I normally ask them to tell us who they are, occupation, family, something unique about themselves, their church background, any prior experience in groups, and perhaps their spiritual journey (in some instances when the group members are new Christians or absolute strangers, I wait until introductions have been completed and then go back for a "second round" to share personal matters like their salvation experience and walk with the Lord. Be sensitive to your group concerning this alternate approach. This is a lot of information and takes time, but it is time well spent.

Some groups like to use games or "ice breakers" to facilitate their introductions. Serendipity's *Beginnings Series* is especially good at this option. The idea is to engage the members in fun activities designed to help them relax and get to know each other. I like this option, but not all group members feel comfortable participating in such activities. You might want to ask the members their opinions before utilizing this option.

As you can imagine, group size has a significant impact on the time it takes to complete all the introductions. Smaller groups of three to eight members may only need one meeting or even less time, depending on the type of group. Larger groups of ten to fifteen members may require up to three meetings. I've been in several groups that even took longer, mainly because during the first few weeks we kept adding new members and had to introduce ourselves over again several times to ensure everyone knew everyone else. Yet regardless of how many meetings you invest in introductions, it is time well spent. Skimping on this process isn't wise.

MAKING SURE EVERYONE IS ABOARD

Have you noticed that every time you board an airplane the flight attendant announces where the plane is going, just to make sure you are on the right flight? I have a friend who didn't pay attention once and ended up in a city far from where he intended to go. He was upset with himself—and embarrassed by the mix-up, not to mention the extra dollars it took him to get to his intended destination. He knew better.

Few people want to go on a trip if they don't know where they are going. As you would expect, small group members fit into this same mindset. They are reluctant to participate in a group they know nothing about. Therefore, it is imperative for you to make certain everyone is on board and knows where the group is headed.

Once all the introductions are completed, the next few meetings must focus on clarifying the group's purpose and goals. This critical information sets the group on the right track and increases its ability to succeed. Lacking this knowledge, members cannot clarify in their own thinking why they are in the group or even if they should be in the group in the first place.

Your personal introduction may have already alerted the mem-

bers to the group's purpose and goals, especially if these are predetermined matters. If this is true, you merely have to review what you
said and spend one meeting exploring the implications and answering any further questions. If the group is free to determine its own
course of action, it may take two or three meetings to discuss and
decide on the specifics. As the leader, you are responsible to facilitate
this process. Be careful not to impose your own ideas on the group.
Yes, you are a group member and have the right to participate. But
your role as leader, especially during these early meetings, may
intimidate some members and prevent them from speaking their
minds or cause them to think what you say is the law. Use persuasive
logic to win their agreement, not bully tactics. Still, once in a while
you must let them do it their way even if the decision doesn't sit well
with you. Give it a chance. If later it proves a poor decision, you can
help them make whatever adjustments are necessary, preferably
without saying "I told you so." The basic aim is to promote group
"ownership" among the members. It must become "our" group, not
"your" (the leader's) group.

To nurture the group's decision-making process, I find it helpful to prepare a simple handout that lists the various decisions
needing resolution and maybe even some options for their consideration. Let me list for you some possible areas or issues the group
must consider. Add to or subtract from the list as appropriate to
your specific situation.

- Purpose and goals
- Size (how many members?)
- Membership (who is "eligible" to join the group?)
- Open or fixed (closed) membership; can new members join at
  any time?
- When to meet
- Where to meet
- Meeting format and agenda
- Meeting leadership (shared or just one person?)
- Group resources (book, study guide, and so on)
- Child care
- Covenant (I talk about this at this chapter's conclusion)

DEFINING THE TOUR STANDARDS

The travel brochure we received outlined our entire trip to Israel, including abundant fine print stipulating everything expected from all the participants. There were "rules" governing the trip. Likewise, your group needs "rules" to operate smoothly. Rarely called rules, more often they are referred to as group norms, standards, or something similar. But whatever they're called, they represent common expectations shared by all the group members and define how they are expected to treat one another. Norms can be either formal or informal in nature.

Our culture operates with often unspoken behavioral norms. For example, don't stand too close to a person when speaking to him or her, don't cut in line, shouting at salesclerks is impolite, don't stare, and so on. Similar informal norms also are at work when you participate in a group setting: be polite and listen, don't interrupt, don't verbally attack people, stay awake, avoid bodily noises, and so on. The only problem with informal norms is that some people don't know what they are and routinely violate such expectations. Then too, disagreements are possible when I act one way and you think it's rude. We disagree, but who's right?

As leader you begin to influence group norms from the minute the members arrive. Even before the official beginning, the other members watch what you do and form opinions on what is and isn't acceptable. You informally demonstrate correct attitudes and behavior. And while this is good, you must not allow norms to exist merely at this informal level. Effective groups talk about their norms and in doing so establish clear, defined behavioral expectations.

Your group shouldn't leave its norms to chance. Often by the third meeting, after spending the first two meetings getting to know each other, the group is ready to talk about what norms they want to adopt. It needn't be a lengthy discussion. In my experience, most groups need only one or two meetings to accomplish this vital mission. Yet don't feel rushed; take as many meetings as necessary to ensure that everyone feels comfortable with the norms you identify.

To assist the "norming" process, once again I usually come to the meeting prepared to share some suggested norms the group may wish to adopt, providing copies for everyone. The members are free to add, subtract, or alter my ideas as they see fit. My desire is to merely prime the pump, not dictate the results. The aim is to come up with a list everyone can support and accept, even though one or two people may not totally agree with every specific norm.

Many more are possible, but here are a few norms to start your brain whirling:

1. *Affirmation and acceptance are important.* Members agree that all the group members are needed in the group. No one is more important; each is accepted for who and what he or she is.

2. *Feelings are legitimate and respected.* Members' feelings are acknowledged, respected, and not belittled.

3. *Honesty is required.* Members promise to be honest with each other, and to avoid half-truths or misleading actions.

4. *Confidentiality is expected.* Members acknowledge that what is said or done in the group remains in the group.

5. *Feedback is welcomed.* Members seek to provide and are willing to receive verbal feedback from one another, but always in a courteous and discerning manner.

6. *Caring behavior is imperative.* Members agree to care for one another by encouragement and by watching out for each other's welfare.

7. *Prayer is appreciated.* Members pledge to pray for one another on a regular basis outside the regular group meetings.

8. *Disagreement is acceptable.* Members acknowledge the right to disagree without being disagreeable.

9. *Speaking for oneself is mandatory.* Members recognize they must speak only for themselves and avoid committing or representing other group members without their approval.

10. *Assisting one another is encouraged.* Members consent to provide time, talent, or financial resources to assist other group members as need may arise.

The norms listed above are "relational" norms, that is, criteria directing how group members treat each other—their interpersonal relationships. Many other behavioral norms are possible. For example, attendance is required, punctuality is important, decisions affecting the group require group approval, unexpected guests are discouraged, children aren't welcome (but this is said more nicely), and everyone needs to leave by 9:30 P.M. (or whatever time is appropriate).

Don't go overboard in putting your list together. I recommend you only include norms the group considers absolutely necessary. Also consider writing down the norms. Doing so makes it much easier to monitor your mutual expectations and evaluate your progress. Just ask someone to serve as your scribe and take notes. Hand out copies at your next meeting.

The norming process itself is as important as the product (norms) it produces. It serves as an excellent team-building activity, uniting the group, enabling the group to begin to think and act like a group. Therefore, keep your attention focused on the process. It is easy to forget your leadership role and get sidetracked by the discussion. Making certain the members experience a mutually satisfying process—based on good communication and decision making—is more essential, at least from the leader's perspective, than the norms they select.

REVIEWING THE FINAL DESTINATION

A tour goes somewhere; it has a destination. There may be intermediate stops along the way, but ultimately you're headed someplace, somewhere specific. I've never been on a trip where we just got into a car or plane and headed out with no final destination in mind. You might enjoy a casual Sunday afternoon outing just wandering about, but rarely does this happen when guests are traveling with you. Small groups are no different.

In my thinking, every group, regardless of type, has a twofold goal or destination: its purpose for existing (the kind of group, its goals and objectives) and the promotion of "community" among its members. Christian community is perhaps the more important general goal.

Christian community is an exciting concept and practice. Believers are not meant to live solitary lives. We're bound together by our faith in Christ. Beginning with a personal relationship with Jesus Christ, every believer is a member of Christ's body, the church.

This corporate relationship is designed to glorify God, strengthen the individual, build our unity, and proclaim the good news of the gospel so everyone has the opportunity to trust in Christ as his or her Savior.

I'm big on small groups because community is best facilitated and realized in small groups. A small group is the ideal context for members to help each other learn and practice what it means to be Christians. Consequently, we must view small groups as more than an optional program, method, or gimmick. They provide a vital context for the body of Christ to function. In fact, I argue that small groups are the most common ministry context or method pictured in Scripture. Check it out for yourself.

If small groups are a key factor in Christian community — the functioning, healthy church or body of Christ — it logically follows we must do everything within our abilities to ensure they succeed. So as I've said before, your leadership role within a group centers on cultivating and nourishing this success.

What does a successful group look like, at least in general terms? You need to develop your own descriptive list, which fits your particular group. However, here is a generic list to get you started. A successful group is characterized as possessing the following characteristics:

- A definable membership—Criteria, if any, for group membership are understood and members know who is in the group. The group has a defined identity.
- Clearly articulated purpose and shared goals—The reason the group exists and what it hopes to accomplish are understood and accepted by all members. A sense of purpose and direction undergird the group.
- Effective communication—Personal and interpersonal communication (verbal and nonverbal) is marked by openness, honesty, courtesy and respect.
- Interdependent and mutually supportive relationships— Members rely on one another and enjoy mutually beneficial relationships. A strong sense of acceptance and belonging is shared among the members.
- Productive meetings—Most members think the group meetings are effective and satisfying. No one feels the meetings waste their time.

- Unity in decision making—While the members may not always agree on a particular issue, they agree to disagree and find the best alternative. Members avoid "blocking" decisions and attempt to support final decisions made by the whole group.

Everything we covered in this chapter is important and cannot be left to chance. Your group must establish relationships, review its purpose, identify its norms, and clarify any operational details. Accomplishing all these things is a challenging but doable task. No one said being a group leader was easy. The first few meetings set the pace and, Lord willing, start the group out on its journey toward becoming a real group.

Here's a tip you mustn't ignore: it's the best method to organize the group's purpose, goals, norms, and the organizational and administrative details. Ready? *Use a group covenant.* A covenant is a written agreement between the members, which stipulates what the members mutually agree upon as fellow travelers, as members in the same group.

Called a "group contract" in some circles, the term "covenant" is a biblical term that seems more appropriate for small groups sponsored by churches and other religious organizations. Call it either name, but use it! No other single tool has more potential for helping your group clarify its existence and set out on the path to success.

For more information about formulating and using a group covenant, see *How to Build a Small Groups Ministry.*

TAKING ACTION

1. Describe the process you plan to use to get your group started off on the right foot.

2. List three things you want to do to help the group members "find their seat."

3. Outline the process you plan to use to assist the group in identifying or clarifying their purpose and goals.

4. To prime the pump and get the group thinking about group norms, identify three norms you recommend that the group consider adopting.

5. Are you prepared to help your group develop a group covenant? If not, what must you do to get ready?

CHAPTER FIVE

The Journey's Challenges

Friends love through all kinds of weather,
and families stick together in all kinds of trouble.
Proverbs 17:17, *The Message*

E VERY trip has its unique challenges, events, or people that tax everyone's patience and test the leader's skill. During my family's trip to Israel we confronted numerous challenges associated with traveling in a foreign country. Being foreigners, we didn't always know the right thing to say or do. Thankfully, nothing we encountered was overwhelming.

As your group journey proceeds you're likely to face a few challenges along the way. It's normal. Consequently, this short chapter deals with several specific "opportunities" to stretch your leadership, occurrences that all too often cause the group to get sidetracked and to stumble on the road to becoming a true group. We need to briefly consider these issues before resuming our discussion on group development.

Ignoring challenges and hoping they go away is one response. It's a favorite method in many churches. Yet it is a foolish alternative. In most cases, ignoring problems just causes them to fester and grow into more difficult situations. No, the best thing to do is step up and seek the best resolution. Let's consider some options to resolving potential challenges you'll face on the journey to becoming a group.

STOP FOR DIRECTIONS

Men often are accused of being unwilling to stop and ask for directions. I'll let you debate whether or not this accusation is accurate.

Anyway, at times it is necessary to stop and get your bearings, to figure out the best road to travel or where you missed the turn. Ideally, such actions aren't needed, but this is wishful thinking. Small groups are a human endeavor which bubble over in their capacity for problems. Problems are fostered by many factors, especially interpersonal relationships. So what alternatives do we have?

In my thinking, the best way to solve problems in a group is to prevent them from occurring in the first place. I know this is idealistic, but it's worth a try and, in my opinion, doable. Don't wait until you have to stop for directions. Take preventive action. On a regular basis set aside time during a meeting to talk about being a group. That's right, spend time discussing what is going on in the group as a group, its processes and relationships.

I call this whole process "formative evaluation." The aim is to discuss and make decisions about your small group's relationships, processes, and activities while there is still time to make any needed or desired changes. It is a positive approach to dealing with situations that if left unaddressed could develop into major headaches.

There are no guarantees, of course, that formative evaluation will work and you'll avoid rough waters. Occasionally, something will pop up or fall apart even when you took pains to defuse the situation. For example, one group I was in identified our need to provide better care for our children during our meetings. After much discussion we came up with several ideas to resolve the problem. Nevertheless, after trying various alternatives, we never found a method that was satisfactory for everyone. Babysitting ended up being a constant hassle and diverted the group members' energy. Ultimately, the group never became a true group because we couldn't resolve this seemingly simple problem.

Various methods are possible, when stopping for directions, to implement formative evaluation. Several alternatives are considered in the next chapter (see *"Rest Stop"*) when we apply the concept to our discussion on developing "real" groups.

MR. AND MRS. TROUBLE

People are potential problems. This isn't news. Every trip has one or two people who cause more than their share of headaches for the leader and fellow travelers. Oh sure, administrative issues can cause a challenge or two during a trip, but the biggest difficulties usually stem from unique personalities, selfishness, and interpersonal conflicts. Don't be surprised if you find yourself investing a lot of time dealing with such issues and the resulting fallout.

Dealing with Mr. or Mrs. Trouble requires patience and dependence on God. You simply cannot do it on your own. No matter how well developed your people skills are, you must lean on the Holy Spirit for wisdom. I am encouraged by the fact that God is patient with me. I must in turn practice this divine attribute and be patient with my group members, which is much easier said than done.

Just as groups don't develop instantly, your people problems or "opportunities" aren't quickly solved by waving a magic wand. A strategy thought out in advance on possible options is a good idea. But even so, it doesn't guarantee 100 percent success. Sometimes God chooses to allow circumstances to form and exist that are beyond your understanding and ability to fix. Nevertheless, as the group leader you need to anticipate encountering difficult group members and be prepared to deal with any situation as it arises.

Each person and situation presents unique challenges. Here are a few things to think about and to help you develop a workable strategy when dealing with difficult people.

1. Deal with the situation as soon as possible; waiting may cause the problem to expand.
2. Accept the person, and make certain they know they have your acceptance, even though you may not agree with what he or she is doing or saying.
3. Find the right time to approach the person; calling them down during a group meeting rarely works (but on a rare, extreme occasion this may be necessary).
4. Find something about them to affirm (for example, they attend regularly, are cheerful, can balance a chair on their chin, and so forth).
5. Stay positive, avoiding condemning words or behavior; even bad situations can be approached positively.
6. Be honest, specific, and straightforward—in a tactful manner—about what attitudes or behaviors are causing difficulties.

7. Ask for change; help them determine what they must do to think or behave in a more acceptable manner.

8. Be patient; allow them adequate time to correct their attitudes and behavior.

9. Affirm their positive response and efforts to make the necessary adjustments.

10. Consider asking the individual to leave the group if he or she refuses to cooperate; this is a last-resort move after every other alternative is exhausted.

A group covenant, a tool I mentioned in the previous chapter, often wards off people problems before they happen. Since everyone participated in the covenanting process and determining the group's norms, no one can say he or she didn't know what was expected. Or at least that's how it's supposed to work. Don't be surprised if it doesn't wrap up so neatly. People have a way of either forgetting or ignoring some things. Besides, many group members don't even know they are causing problems. Only after you approach them do they realize they are causing difficulties.

Don't be shy. Ask for help if you find you cannot deal with a group member who resists all your attempts to deal with his or her unproductive attitudes or behaviors. Your pastor or small group ministry leader will usually help you deal with the situation. Bringing someone in from the outside often provides solutions that were evasive up to that point.

FLAT TIRE

We sat quietly on our tour bus while the giant tire was changed. The trip was delayed for two hours and we didn't make it to the next tourist site before it closed. No one was to blame. The bus driver didn't see the nail in the road. Still, the flat tire had derailed our journey for that day.

On occasion your group will experience a "flat tire," something that happens that is beyond your control, something that just occurs. Frequently, group development is halted until the flat is fixed. You can attempt to keep going by driving on a flat tire, but it isn't recommended. The best option is to fix the problem and resume your journey.

In some cases you fix a flat by taking off the punctured tire and replacing it with a spare tire. In a group context, this means finding a suitable alternative or changing directions. Let's say you start out meeting on Tuesday evenings. After eight weeks, three couples find that their schedules no longer allow them to meet on Tuesdays. You have a choice. Go on without them or change the day you meet. Since six people are involved, potentially half the group, it is wisest to find a new day to meet. This alternative is especially applicable if the group has met together on a weekly basis for more than two months. By this time the group members have invested significant time and energy in getting started. Disbanding or going on without the couples who face schedule changes would waste valuable momentum.

One more example: Suppose you, the group leader, move. You didn't plan it this way, but your spouse is offered a big promotion, one that requires a move to Pittsburgh. It's something your family cannot pass up. Now what? Does your group find a new leader or just disband? How glorious for you if the group concluded it could not go on without you, but you know it's not true. The best choice is to change the tire—find a new leader. And even though they will miss you, ideally someone in the group assumes the role and the group moves forward.

Another alternative for fixing a flat is to remove the tire, repair the puncture, put it back on, and resume your trip. For your group this means stopping to make needed adjustments to current methods or practices and then continuing on. Dropping the administrative procedure, scrapping the activity, or taking some other terminal action isn't necessary. Simple repairs are all that's needed.

A group I formerly was in set a goal to spend one meeting per month practicing our "body responsibilities" (helping other church members). We wanted to help older members with tasks or seasonal chores around their homes. It was a terrific idea, but it was a small new church and we didn't have many older members. We experienced difficulty in contacting the older members, scheduling appropriate tasks, and finding times that worked for everyone. It was frustrating. Rather than abandon the idea altogether, we talked it over and widened our target area and sought to assist people in all age brackets and even not-for-profit, faith-based organizations. This simple repair to our "flat tire" worked well.

A "repair approach" to your group's operation is wise. There is no need to feel you must stick with every decision you or the group made in the early stages. Be willing to flex. Adjustments are good if they assist the group in becoming a group and achieving its purpose and goals.

Here are some guidelines to help you when your group experiences a "flat tire."

1. Praise the Lord. Your first reaction is to thank the Lord for the opportunity to depend on Him. Every situation has a purpose in God's overall plan, even if you don't understand what it is at the moment. (James 1:2-4)

2. Stay calm; getting all excited doesn't help the situation. The group members depend on you, their leader, to set the pace.

3. Pray about it. Too often, prayer is our last response. Make certain you are praying about the situation from the very beginning. (Philippians 4:6)

4. Ask God for wisdom in dealing with the matter. Remind yourself that God is the real group leader and you are only His assistant. What does He want you to do? (James 1:5)

5. Talk it over as a group. The best solutions are usually ones that come from the whole group deliberating on the issue or problem. After all, it's also their group!

6. Be willing to try something different. It may be necessary to implement a different action, change directions, or find an alternative route.

7. Don't drive on risky roads. If you know an administrative decision, program format, or anything else is treacherous for your group, perhaps it's wise to avoid flirting with danger. After all, discretion is the better part of valor.

One last comment about changing a "flat tire". In some cases you may have to check with your pastor or some other ministry leader before you alter or drop any group practices. It's not uncommon for some churches to require certain methods, actions, or activities for all their groups. Leaders and group members aren't free to make any adjustments they deem necessary. If your group is part of a larger, highly structured groups ministry, you need to clear any adjustments prior to their implementation.

WRONG TURN

"Turn left!"

"No," the guide insisted, "we need to go right." So the bus turned right—after all, he was the tour guide and should have known where we were going. Bad call! Turning right, we ended up on a dead-end street with not enough room to turn the bus around.

Like the tour guide, you as the group leader are bound to make a wrong call once in a while. It goes with the job. No one expects perfection from you (expect perhaps you). Making mistakes is a human frailty we all must accept, even in our role as a group leader.

Sometimes difficult circumstances just happen, but all too often we find ourselves in hot water or an uncomfortable predicament because of what we said or did, or perhaps what we didn't say or do. We rarely would choose such complications. Frequently our inexperience is the root cause of our problems. As you gain experience in leading a group, the blunders are reduced—but they never go away totally.

Mistakes usually happen with greater frequency when the group is first starting. You and the other members are getting to know one another, trying to figure out the best group practices, and experimenting with administrative details. A few unintentional errors during this initial phase is normal. How you deal with these inevitable challenges is the real question. Handling them in a correct fashion is imperative.

When you make a mistake—and you will—keep these things in mind as you deal with the situation:

1. Be quick to admit your mistakes, whether the errors are large or small. In some circumstances you may have to ask a group member or the whole group for forgiveness.
2. Avoid lame excuses or trying to blame someone else. Admitting you made a mistake but then hedging with a "he-made-me-do-it" or "it's-really-not-my fault" excuse isn't a mature response. If you did it, you did it.
3. Accept the responsibility to make any necessary corrections or mend any broken fences. Saying you're sorry or admitting the mistake is a good start, but you also have to correct any "damage" that may have occurred.

4. Determine how to avoid repeating the mistake. A wise leader learns from making mistakes and works strenuously to avoid making the same error a second time.
5. In truly extreme cases, be willing to step aside and have the group select a new leader. Usually this drastic step isn't even considered. However, if the group's well-being or corporate testimony is hindered by your continuing leadership, be forthright in relinquishing your leadership role.

Take comfort in the fact that you're not the only one in the group who can trip up. Naturally, other members or the group as a whole also can make mistakes. When this occurs it's vital for you to remain positive and treat the situation with kid gloves. How you react is important. Avoid making a big deal over the error or dwelling on the blunder. Do whatever is necessary to correct the fumble, but once it's resolved, move on and forget the incident.

Caution! Don't allow yourself to develop an "it's okay" excuse pattern. Just because it's normal for you or the group to make errors in judgement or actions, it's not acceptable to do things haphazardly and then repeatedly brush off the mistakes as being normal. If you fall into this faulty routine, your group may never achieve your or the group's expectations.

ABANDON SHIP

Tired and exhausted, the travelers gave up and returned home. They had tried. Nothing went as planned. They missed their flight because the tickets were not at the airline counter as promised, one traveler came down with chicken pox, another member failed to show up at all, some luggage was stolen off the curb, and to top it off, when they tried to contact the travel agency they were informed it had just filed for bankruptcy and the owner had disappeared with all their money. Quitting seemed like their only alternative. No trip this time.

Put yourself in their place. If you were a part of this ill-fated group, your response may have been similar. The time may come when, after all your efforts, you or the other small group members feel like calling it quits and abandoning ship. Careful, caution is warranted. You and your group should view quitting as the last option, a choice to be made only after you try everything else. Don't take the easy way out. Seldom is quitting the only alternative.

Let's be real. Even though we may not like to admit it, on rare occasions the best thing to do is to end the group. I'm sure other possibilities exist, but here are several reasons for which I have seen groups end their journey.

- After numerous attempts, the group members aren't able to agree on a day, time, and\or place to meet. It seems every option ends up excluding half the group.
- The group members are too different from one another. Age, background, or some other factor prevents the group members from feeling comfortable with each other. This shouldn't be the case, but occasionally this variable becomes an insurmountable obstacle.
- An interpersonal breach occurs and the members elect to stop meeting. While extremely unusual, a group may become so traumatized by a horrific event (such as a terrible crime, gross moral failure, or serious breach of confidentiality) that they lose the desire to meet with one another.
- The group has met for many years and decides to call it quits. Routine and boredom have set in. Members miss meetings frequently. No one is angry; everyone just feels like it is time for a change. Most members express interest in being in another group, now or in the near future.
- A majority of the members move, change churches, or for whatever reason can no longer attend.
- One last reason I'll mention really doesn't fit here, but I need to mention it anyway. The group concludes because it reaches the predetermined ending point. Many groups covenant to meet together for specific periods of time—six weeks, six months, one year, and so on. Deciding to quit isn't difficult because it is considered normal in the group's life cycle. In fact, under these circumstances it isn't viewed as "quitting" at all. Rather, it is seen as completing the journey. New journeys are on the horizon.

Making the decision to quit is difficult. Be sure everyone in the group participates in the decision-making process. Leave no one out. Moreover, you may find it helpful and even necessary to prolong the decision over several meetings while other options are explored. It's never a good idea to call it quits on a moment's notice.

Be prepared to deal with emotions. Depending on the reasons behind why the group is thinking about stopping, there may be some highly charged, emotional meetings. Ideally, all the group members can weather these intense storms. But occasionally one or more members cannot handle emotional or interpersonal tension and merely drop out without "processing" the decision with the other group members. If this occurs, you may need to go talk with the individuals and, with their permission, state their views at subsequent meetings in their absence. In any event, don't deny or disparage emotions. Help the members express, deal with, and hopefully resolve how they feel.

Is there someone other than the group members who needs to participate in the decision to abort the group, such as a pastor or ministry leader? Does your church already have an established policy on how a group goes about ending? Most churches don't, but you need to inquire and follow any existing procedures. Concluding a group in a decent and orderly manner is just as important as starting and properly running a small group.

After the decision to stop meeting is made, it's important to do so in a caring, systematic fashion. You may want to have a final farewell meeting or dinner to reminisce about the good times. Having a picnic or going to an amusement park together are also possibilities. The intent is to leave the members with a good feeling about the group even though the circumstances causing the breakup may be less than positive. Of course, in really "hot" situations it may be best to forgo a final meeting and just write a thank-you letter to all the members.

My purpose in this chapter was to deal briefly with some common challenges you may face on the journey toward helping your group become a real group. I wish I could make the journey easy and trouble-free for you, but unfortunately I cannot. Just remember to practice this biblical admonition:

Consider it a sheer gift, friends, when tests and challenges come at you from all sides. You know that under pressure, your faith-life is forced into the open and shows its true colors. So don't try to get out of anything prematurely. Let it do its work so you become mature and well-developed, not deficient in any way. If you don't know what you're doing, pray to the Father. He loves to help. You'll get his help, and won't be condescended to when you ask for it. James 1:2-5, (MSG)

TAKING ACTION

1. Thinking about your group, what challenges are you likely to face (or have you already faced)?

2. Describe how you would approach a member who tends to dominate your group conversations.

3. Planning ahead is wise. Identify a potential "flat tire" your group could encounter and what you can do to help group members avoid the situation.

4. Oops! You made a big mistake. Some members weren't informed that the meeting was canceled, and six people showed up anyway. As the leader, how would you handle this predicament?

5. Describe the conditions or situation that would cause you to consider "abandoning ship" and ending the group. What would you do if the situation you describe actually occurred?

CHAPTER SIX

Almost There

Without good direction, people lose their way;
the more wise counsel you follow, the better your chances.
Proverbs 11:14, *The Message*

W E'RE almost there. A brief stopover at Amsterdam and then
on to Israel. As we near our destination, our anticipation
increases. Spending two weeks in Israel is an exciting prospect that is
about to come true. The journey continues.

Your group isn't a real group yet, but it's getting closer; you're
almost there. At this point in your journey you should begin seeing
the developing possibilities. Increasing glimpses of your group's
potential to become a mature group provide both excitement and the
encouragement to keep pressing on. Your destination—a fully-
functioning group—is within sight. Your time and energy invested
thus far are about to pay off, Lord willing.

In chapter 4 we explored issues related to the first two stages in
group development, *birth and infancy* and *childhood.* Now we turn
our attention to your group's intermediate developmental stage,
teenager. No longer a child and not yet an adult, the teenage period is
marked by self-examination, conforming to expectations, questioning, adjustments, and perhaps a little turmoil. It's a time of emer-
gence when attitudes and behavior move from immaturity to
maturity. Thankfully, once your group has processed successfully
through its teenage issues the group members are ready to begin
functioning like a real group.

In terms of our journey, the teenage stage represents a period in
the group's development where its members are moving closer to the

ideal "we," "us," and "our" mindset, away from their individualism, and toward seeing the group as "theirs." "Groupness" is on the verge of taking full root and blooming: all that's necessary is to weather the teenage phase.

THE JOURNEY THUS FAR

Have you noticed that even before a trip is over, people begin to think and talk about what they've experienced up to that point. Already they are beginning to build memories. Groups are really no different. By the time your group has met for ten or more weeks (assuming weekly meetings), a healthy group has already begun to tell stories and joke about their early meetings. How much this occurs depends on the individual group and how well it is progressing.

Not all groups move easily into their teenage stage. Some struggle for many weeks at the earlier stages. All small groups, like humans, do not develop at the same rate. If your group seems like it is slow in developing, be patient. Some groups are just late bloomers.

Ideally, your group's teenage stage has begun if many of the following characteristics are true:

- Members know each other's names, personal facts, and when appropriate to the type of group, personal stories and spiritual journeys.
- A group covenant was developed and now guides the group's actions.
- Administrative issues (when, what, how, and so on) are fairly well settled and operating.
- Membership and participation are stabilizing.
- Your role as leader is established among the members.
- A group "spirit" is taking hold and individualism is decreasing.
- Members are beginning to talk with friends about "their group."
- A few "trouble spots" in relationships, format, or agenda are starting to emerge.
- Individual members may be experiencing some doubts or reservations about the group in general and their ongoing participation in specific.

- Trust among the members has reached a level where they feel comfortable sharing their ideas and opinions.
- The group is well on its way to assuming shared leadership.

It's unlikely your small group is hitting 100 percent in all the areas I just listed. Hopefully, however, the majority of these characteristics describe your group. If not, I advise you to identify the ones that need the most work and explore how to improve in these areas before forging ahead in the group developmental process. This remedial action isn't always easy. Figuring out what to do depends on your ability to read the signs your group is displaying. Unfortunately, since every group is unique and the options are many, I cannot suggest an exact course for you to follow. Nevertheless, there is a formal process, which can be very helpful: formative evaluation, our next topic.

REST STOP

It's normal to take rest stops. When my family travels by auto we usually stop every three or four hours to stretch, buy gas, get something to drink, and check the map to make certain we are heading in the right direction. Our brief stops invigorate us, and we're ready to continue on. It's also smart for your small group to take occasional rest stops during your journey together.

In chapter 5 we were introduced to formative evaluation—a systematic process to make decisions about the group's relationships, processes, and activities while the group is still forming and time remains to make any needed changes or adjustments. (*How to Build a Small Groups Ministry* contains a general overview of this subject.) Just keep in mind that the evaluation process you're dealing with at this juncture takes place while the group is still meeting and is intended to help you to determine *how the group is doing* thus far, to identify any needed changes or adjustments, and to prepare the group for proceeding on. In chapter 8 we'll talk about a "summative" evaluation, a final process just prior to the group's conclusion to determine *how things went.*

With your group moving into its teenager phase, now is an

excellent time for your first serious attempt at formative evaluation. Up to this point you have dealt with various issues as they have arisen naturally during the group's beginning stages. With the Holy Spirit's direction, you and the group members together were able to resolve the various problems you faced. The time has come for you to set aside some portion of a group meeting to reflect on what has taken place thus far and determine if there is anything you need to do to facilitate your continuing development.

There are many ways to conduct a group's formative evaluation (some group leaders prefer to use the term "assessment" or "progress assessment"). Here is a simple four-step example you might want to consider. It is an informal approach, but more rigorous methods are possible. Make any adjustments you think are necessary if you use the process with your specific group.

A SIMPLE FOUR-STEP FORMATIVE EVALUATION MODEL	
STEP ONE	Pre-evaluation; introducing formative evaluation; planning the process
STEP TWO	Conducting the evaluation; gathering the "information"
STEP THREE	Making decisions; deciding what to do
STEP FOUR	Implementing results; making needed adjustments or changes

Step One—Pre-evaluation; introducing formative evaluation. The
first thing you need to do is alert the members. Several weeks before
the meeting at which you intend to conduct the formative evaluation
(select a meeting sometime after your tenth meeting) very briefly
introduce the basic concept. Explain that the members need to stop
for a few minutes at an upcoming meeting and talk about how they
are doing as a group. Make sure they understand it isn't a gripe session. Rather, the purpose is to identify things the group is doing well
and should continue doing, areas that may need some adjustments,
and elements that appear to need total rethinking and perhaps
change.

Sometimes a group isn't ready for a thorough formative evaluation. They haven't reached a point in their group development where
familiarity and trust are firmly established. There is no magic for-
mula for determining this readiness. Every small group is different,
and only you can judge if your group is ready. Let's assume the time
is right—a majority of the characteristics listed previously are present—and you decide to proceed.

At the meeting just preceding the designated meeting at which
you plan to conduct the evaluation, introduce the concept to the
group members in greater detail. Describe the process you have in
mind. Be as specific as you can (the following steps give you this
information). Ask them to begin thinking about how the group can
improve in four areas:

1. *Administrative details*—For example, day, time, place, child
   care
2. *Format and agenda*—What the group does when it meets,
   time structure, and so on
3. *Relationships*—Identification, trust, openness, caring, communication, and acceptance among the members
4. *Leadership*—Your planning, leading activities, helping the
   group make decisions, personal style, or any area of concern
   (This is the most difficult area for most leaders. After all, it
   deals with your leadership performance. Don't balk. It may be
   hard, but you need to include this factor in the assessment.
   Work hard at not becoming defensive or making excuses if
   something less than positive is suggested by the members.)

You might consider excluding relationships and leadership if you don't think the group is able to deal with these more sensitive issues at this point. They can be included later in subsequent formative evaluations. For now it may be best to deal with the more factual, routine issues related to the group's operating details and format. On the other hand, your group may be ready to deal with all four areas listed above. Let's suppose this is the case.

One final pre-evaluation task remains: planning how you want to conduct the actual evaluation. For our current example, let's consider using a very basic strategy—open discussion. This assumes the group has achieved a comfort level with each other that permits open and frank verbal communication. More complicated approaches—interviews, checklists, questionnaires, rating scales—are sometimes beneficial when a comfort level isn't fully present and the members are hesitant to openly express themselves.

Since we are going to use a discussion as our assessment strategy, you would be smart to write out your questions beforehand. Keep the questions short and sweet. If the group has really struggled up to this point, you may want to use numerous questions, but more commonly one or two questions per evaluation area are satisfactory.

Asking open-ended questions (questions that cannot be answered yes or no) is your best bet. Below are four extremely basic open-ended questions, which fit our present example. They are designed to stimulate discussion and perhaps even raise additional questions.

1. What administrative details, if any, need to be adjusted or changed?
2. What format or agenda adjustments, if any, are needed?
3. How satisfied are you with the interpersonal relationships within our group?
4. How can I, as our group leader, improve my service to you and the group as a whole?

Is there anything else you need to do to prepare for your formative evaluation? I ask this question because your specific situation may require you to consider other issues before conducting the evaluation. For instance, do you need to use a prescribed evaluation format or instrument provided by your church's small groups ministry leaders? Are there designated times when all groups are expected to engage in progress assessment? Does every member know about the upcoming evaluation? Will a majority of the group members be present at the meeting set aside for doing the evaluation? Is another group member better suited to lead the evaluation process? These and other possible questions represent additional details that may need your attention prior to conducting your first or subsequent evaluations.

When you are certain everything is planned and prepared and you have committed the whole process to God in prayer, you're ready to proceed. The next step occurs at the actual meeting.

Step Two—Conducting the evaluation; gathering the "information." The designated meeting has arrived. After your group's usual preliminary activities, in an upbeat tone turn their attention to the evaluation or progress assessment. Explain again the aim: to stop and assess how the group is doing and identify if there are any needed adjustments or potential changes. Ask for their permission to jot down a few notes as the discussion unfolds. To begin, pray and ask for God's wisdom and the Holy Spirit's leading.

Now you need their input, their opinions on how they think the group is doing. Ask the questions you prepared earlier in Step One. Sometimes it's helpful to write the questions on a poster or prepare a handout and give everyone a copy. Keep in mind the aim for this step is to identify issues, factors, elements, or problems that require adjustment or complete change. I like to use a large piece of paper and write down the issues so everyone can see the areas as they are identified by the group. However, I don't write down anything until everyone agrees it is an issue the group needs to deal with. Securing this agreement is difficult at times. Opinions always vary. So, your group-process skills are important to make the whole procedure work.

Step Two may require only ten to fifteen minutes, but be prepared to take whatever time is necessary for everyone to express an opinion. Rushing to get done might cause the members to conclude that the process or their opinions aren't really important or wanted.

Step Three—Making decisions; deciding what to do. Once you identify the areas needing attention, you must lead the group in determining the appropriate responses. What is needed? Are adjustments or complete change required? Each item identified in Step Two is now considered, and possible alternatives are identified. Pros and cons for each alternative are discussed. Hopefully, an unbiased and logical discussion yields adequate solutions.

Step Three often takes the greatest amount of time during the meeting. While it's somewhat difficult to agree on the issues needing resolution, more frequently the members find it harder to agree on the solutions. Proceed slowly; make sure everyone is willing to accept the final decision. This doesn't mean everyone needs to agree fully. Rather, all the members need to support trying the alternative, adjustment, or suggested change. Reversing the decision or finding a completely different option is possible at a later date.

Occasionally a group finds it necessary to postpone a decision on a specific solution. Thinking and praying about the matter for a week or two is warranted. Relationship and leadership issues frequently fit into this category. If such action is justified, make sure the matter is not forgotten, and ensure appropriate action is taken at some predetermined point.

Some group leaders prefer to identify issues (Step Two) and their solutions (Step Three) simultaneously, rather than as separate steps. This is perfectly acceptable. One caution, however. It's very easy to get bogged down when doing both together. Time slips by, the meeting ends, and some of the issues remain unaddressed. This situation is okay, of course, if the group wishes to invest additional time at the next meeting to complete the process.

Step Four — Implementing results; making needed adjustments or changes. The final step in this simple model is to actually put into practice any identified changes or adjustments. Some of these are easily completed on the spot, at that very meeting; others take careful consideration and cautious implementation over time. If decisions are postponed or take time to implement, be sure to follow up on these details and keep the other members informed. The next major section in this chapter deals with dynamics associated with Step Four in more detail.

To wrap up the evaluation, thank everyone for their participation. Tell them you plan to do a similar process occasionally in order to help the group stay fit and in shape. The group will continue to deal with any "challenges" that may pop up unexpectedly, but every several months you plan to use a small amount of time during a meeting to talk about how the group is doing as a group.

The four steps just outlined are basic. Many other variations are possible. Tailor a process to fit your situation. Don't be shy about adding or subtracting steps. No one but you is best able to judge what your group needs or what is most fitting. Remember, the goal isn't merely to do a formative evaluation, but to conduct a progress assessment that promotes your group's continuing development and success.

As you begin to think about and carry out a formative evaluation with your group, keep these things in mind:

- Formative evaluation works best when the process is saturated in prayer and the whole group seeks the Holy Spirit's direction.

- Formative evaluation must involve all the group members. Doing it on your own outside the group meetings is only acceptable if you bring your observations to the group for further discussion and approval. Much better results are secured when your fellow group members are actively involved in the evaluation process.

- Formative evaluation demands time. Budget adequate time, perhaps a whole group meeting if necessary.

- Formative evaluation is a positive tool to assist you in helping your group, not a club to beat them with. Abstain from using the evaluation to complain about individual group members, to criticize the group when they are reluctant to do what you want, or to chide them if they are slow in developing into a "real" group.

- Formative evaluation is not a one-time event. It must be conducted at regular intervals. It's not unusual for a group to do three or four formative evaluations during each year they meet — in conjunction with the stages of group development.

Having just read about doing a formative evaluation you might argue, "I don't need to do an evaluation, it's a waste of time." You may think this way, but I suggest it's faulty thinking. In reality, formative evaluation is an effort to formalize and capture the greatest benefit from a process that is already going on among your group members. We all evaluate any situation in which we find ourselves. We may not say anything, other than to our spouse, but we routinely size up events, people, programs, or sermons assessing their worth, effectiveness, or ability to interest us. Consequently, use formative evaluation to harness this informal appraisal and turn it into constructive benefit for the group's welfare.

CHANGING THE TRIP'S ITINERARY

It's not unusual to find that a change in your trip's itinerary is needed. Something you planned to do isn't possible. Another previously unknown opportunity comes to your attention. A traveling companion becomes ill and cannot continue on. Your money is gone more quickly than you anticipated. Planned or unplanned events can easily cause a change in the intended calendar and activities. I recall several occasions during my family's trip to Israel when our tour guide called us all together to explain how or why the planned itinerary wasn't going to work and to ask us to select from new alternatives.

Small groups also can face the need to change their itineraries, especially during the teenage stage. Needed adjustments are identified when routine operations don't work, members express concern or dissatisfaction, some other factor is identified by you or the other members, or as we just learned, a formative evaluation identifies something that needs adjustment or change.

Let's pretend your formative evaluation identified four issues: (1) start the group on time; (2) slow down and don't attempt to cover so much material at each meeting; (3) find out why Mel and Sue Taylor haven't attended in the past three weeks; and (4) include another member to share in leading the group meetings. Implementing these needed adjustments or changes is now in order. How you go about doing so is very important. Let me suggest the following:

1. *Start on time* — As you can imagine, solving this issue is relatively straightforward: just start on time from now on. The hard part is actually doing it. As the leader, you are the person who has to make sure this solution is implemented.
2. *Cover less material per meeting* — Apparently the group is

using a book as the basis for its meetings. Help the members determine how much information is reasonable to cover per meeting, let's say half a chapter per week. Based on this decision, formulate a new schedule.

3. *Contact the Taylors*—Why have Mel and Sue been gone for three weeks? Ask if a group member is willing to contact them and find out what's happening and then report back to the group next week. Showing interest in fellow group members is a vital aspect of your group's development.

4. *Share group leadership*—Hopefully you don't take this adjustment too personally. The group's desire to share in leadership responsibilities is a good sign. The group is maturing. Yet, it's doubtful that every group member wants a turn at leading meetings. Identify those who are willing, formulate a schedule, and do whatever is needed to help them succeed. Their success is the group's and your success.

Did you happen to catch the pattern present in the adjustments we just covered? Three elements were present in each situation: *What* to do, *who* does it, and *when* it's done. *How* it's done is secondary, but still important. Any action must be logical, reasonable, considerate, and acceptable to all the group members. *Why* it's done was established earlier during the formative evaluation.

One noteworthy event can significantly alter any group's itinerary: adding new group members. When new members join a group at any point beyond the first three or four weeks, the group essentially starts over as a group; it's a new ball game. Why? Because the group must once again go through the preliminary stages associated with introductions, getting to know each other, and establishing trust. Therefore, be cautious when your group wants to add additional members. Such caution is especially true for relationship-oriented groups.

Adding new members is perfectly acceptable when it fits your group type and purpose, *all* the group members are in agreement, and members recognize the need and are willing to "back up" and go through initial group-building tasks. However, adding a new member may be beyond your control if it is required by your church's small groups ministry leaders. Just don't forget to secure agreement on all three points *before* any new members arrive. Likewise, ideally you already discussed — way back at the beginning when your group first got started — adding new members. It's an important topic when developing your covenant. Doing so avoids any misunderstanding, which might occur if you wait until the teenage stage or later to make the decision on adding members.

BACK ON THE ROAD

The earlier "rest stop" (formative evaluation) hopefully was useful in determining how well your group has developed up until now. After making any needed adjustments or changes, which are common during the teenage phase, the group is back on course moving toward group maturity.

The group's teenage developmental stage, or being "almost there," involves a few additional issues we need to consider. *First*, it's entirely possible your small group has one or two members who are "blocking" the group's development. In other words, their behavior or attitudes are causing the group some problems. Members like this often display one or more of the following characteristics: overly critical, unwilling to cooperate with group decisions, judgmental, moody, demanding, unreliable, betray confidentiality, gossip, withdrawn, overly verbal, domineering, easily offended . . . actually, any of the common maladies that plague people are likely to also plague your group. How do you respond?

Dealing with difficult people can cause you some sleepless nights. Yet, ignoring the bothersome person/situation isn't the answer. You need to take action. Let me make two points: (1) Deal with the person or persons outside the group first. Only make it a group matter if the person is unwilling to change and, when necessary, make amends. (2) Hopefully it won't be necessary, but ultimately you must be ready to ask the person to leave the group if all efforts fail to correct the situation. No one wants this to happen, but in the final analysis the group's well-being takes priority over any individual member. This is my opinion; this isn't an acceptable notion in some people's thinking.

Second, talk about group development often during the teenage phase. Talking helps. Open communication about the group's development nearly always is beneficial. I find group members more willing to endure the bumps along the way when they understand what is happening. I'm not suggesting you or the group dwell on the subject. Merely include the topic in your introductory comments when starting meetings, make it a prayer request, joke about it on occasion, and point out positive progress.

Third, like human teenagers, groups at this stage need reassurance. When a group experiences "growing pains" it's easy to assume everything is falling apart and the group won't succeed. Nothing could be further from the truth. You need to constantly reassure your group that it's normal for all groups to experience turmoil to some greater or lesser degree. It's a healthy stage in becoming a real group. Group conflict, strife, or unrest occur periodically but eventually go away. Becoming mature isn't always an easy road.

Fourth, be patient. Having teenagers is a trying experience. During your group's teen phases you, as the leader, need to exercise extreme patience at all times. You'll find yourself ready to scream, but don't; it doesn't do any good. How you act and react is an important model for the group members. They need to see your forbearance. Ask God to help you "admonish the unruly, encourage the fainthearted, help the weak, be patient with all men" (1 Thessalonians 5:14) and "Bear one another's burdens, and thus fulfill the law of Christ" (Galatians 6:2).

GET OUT AND PUSH

Have you ever been on a car trip where you had to slow down because the road was no longer paved? I remember one time when several friends and I were on a logging road in Oregon. Our journey came to a halt—we were stuck in the mud. We had to get out and push. It took some strenuous effort, but soon we were back on our way. It was only a brief delay.

Don't be surprised if your group is progressing just fine and all of a sudden it seems to slow down and get stuck. Boredom appears, members seem less enthusiastic, attendance becomes sporadic, and a few members even drop out. It's not at all unusual for the "blahs" to occur sometime during the group's later teenage phase. It may cause a brief delay in your group's development, but you can quickly prevail over the problem.

What can you and the group do to overcome the blahs? Perhaps it's time for some variety. The options are endless. Here are some suggestions to spark your creativity:

- If several months have passed since your last progress assessment (formative evaluation), it may be wise to go through the process once again.
- Suspend your regular format and agenda for two or three weeks and do something different (this may be difficult if it's a task-oriented group).
- Have a weekend retreat; get away as a group for fun and relaxation together.
- Change your setting; switch to a new meeting location.
- Find a worthwhile project you can complete together as a group.
- Take a month off (not usually a good idea, but it can work is some cases).
- Meet with another group for several weeks to consider a special topic or subject.
- Volunteer as a group to staff the church nursery for a month.
- Switch to a small group video series for four to six weeks.

In short, don't become alarmed if your group struggles with the blahs. It's a frequent occurrence. I've found it helpful to discuss the issue with the members before it happens and plan some ways to stop it from even occurring. No group wants to get stuck. Be prepared!

Well, we've finished another chapter. Lord willing, your group will progress through its teenage phase and become ready to enter "adulthood." But before you go on to the next chapter, invest a few minutes completing the following Taking Action section.

TAKING ACTION

1. Describe how you conducted or how you plan to conduct your group's first formative evaluation.

2. If you've already done a formative evaluation, what did you discover about your group, and what action did you take?

3. Let's pretend your group identified the need to add four new members to the group. Describe how you would recruit these individuals and what you would do to help them assimilate into the group.

4. Outline a strategy you think might work to deal with a difficult group member.

5. Review the list of suggestions for overcoming group blahs (p. 88) and add two more creative ideas to the list.

CHAPTER SEVEN

Arriving at the Destination

The lives of God-loyal people flourish;
a misspent life is soon bankrupt.
Proverbs 15:6, *The Message*

"**D**AD, we're here!" my daughter exclaimed as we circled over the airport and our plane began its descent to land. It had been a long trip. We were ready to enjoy all the thrills associated with arriving at our destination. We planned to see and do everything possible for two whole weeks.

Don't expect your group to arrive at its "adult" developmental stage with a defining event like landing an airplane. Nonetheless, at some point—ideally after the group has meet for four or five months—your group enters into its fourth phase, what I call "maturity." At this point the group is functioning fairly well and its purpose for existing is being realized. Relational groups are now enjoying strong, mutually beneficial interpersonal relationships; content groups are exploring the biblical or topical depths; task groups are able to accomplish their duties in an effective, efficient manner; and need-based groups are successful in helping the members deal with the issue or need behind the group's existence. Regardless of the specific type of group, the members are now beginning to function at an optimum level.

In this chapter we explore what "maturity" means for small groups. Lord willing, you'll gain some valuable insights into helping your group achieve this desirable phase in a group's life. At this point in the journey your group should be ready to realize its full potential and benefits.

WE'RE HERE

A mature group is the goal, the target you've been aiming at from the very beginning. Yet, recognizing or defining a mature group isn't always straightforward. No two groups are exactly the same. Each group, like a person, has a unique personality and "lifestyle." Describing a fully functioning or mature group eludes neatly packaged descriptions. Nevertheless, here are some generalizations, which can help you discern if and when your group is mature:

- Membership is stable and attendance is regular.
- Group members know and accept one another.
- Members understand, accept, and are working to accomplish the group's purpose and goals.
- The group is able to act as one, to make decisions, to function with minimal friction.
- Verbal interaction among the members is open, honest, frequent, and balanced.
- A group mindset prevails over individual preferences.
- When difficulties arise, they are dealt with and resolved in a sensitive and caring manner.
- The group's agenda or task is balanced with appropriate attention to relationships.
- Members spend time together outside the group meetings.
- Shared leadership is normative; members' dependence on the leader is minimal.
- Administrative details are well established.
- Members express satisfaction with being in the group and about what the group is doing.

The above characteristics are generalizations about group maturity and apply to all types of groups. Rarely, however, does any individual group score 100 percent in all these areas. More often a group is strong in several, rates okay in the majority, and has one or two characteristics that aren't up to speed and need serious attention. Your group is no different. Don't expect perfection.

Let me suggest some specific traits that might help you distinguish maturity within the various types of groups. Of course other characteristics are possible, but the ones listed below are key.

Relationship (or process) groups
1. A creative format and agenda capitalize on building relationships.
2. Flexibility exists to set aside a planned activity in order to assist with a member's needs.
3. Effort is made by the members to encourage and help one another.
4. "Our" group takes priority over members' individual preferences.

Content groups
1. Lively discussion occurs without anyone dominating the conversation.
2. Mutual agreement is reached among members when selecting content, topic, or text.
3. Members demonstrate a willingness to disagree without being disagreeable.
4. Relationships are warm and cordial, even though they're not the focal point.

Task groups
1. A "one-for-all-and-all-for-one" spirit permeates the group.
2. Members focus on the shared task, but do not neglect interpersonal relationships.
3. Intentional processes are utilized to accomplish the task and reach goals.
4. Members are patient and helpful with less-experienced group members.

Need-based groups
1. Definite "ground rules" (norms) are understood and accepted by all members.
2. New members are quickly assimilated into the group.
3. A non-judgmental, supportive, no-nonsense attitude is present.
4. Members feel the group helps them deal with the issues under consideration.

A mature, well-functioning group is a delight to behold and participate in. Hopefully this phase is the group's longest, lasting five, six, or more months (assuming the group has covenanted to meet for one year). But a word of caution is in order. Group maturity isn't a plateau, a status to reach, which then remains fixed and unchanging. On the contrary, a group is dynamic and susceptible to fluctuations. We are talking about a human endeavor, after all. People change. Likewise, groups change. What is true today might become very different tomorrow.

Given a group's dynamic nature, maintaining its mature phase requires focused, ongoing effort on your part. You cannot just assume everything will continue on uninterrupted. Leading a mature group is easier than leading a less-developed group, but you must still attend to certain functional details. Here's a list of things you need to continuing caring for during the group's mature phase:

1. Coordinate events and people—It's likely the group's mature phase will necessitate you switching gears and assuming a coordinating role rather than an up-front leadership role. Someone must make sure that the who, what, when, where, and why associated with the group's meetings, activities, events, and session leaders are actualized. You are that person. Even when you delegate these "behind-the-scenes" tasks, you still retain overall accountability. Moreover, as leader you are the group's communication hub, making sure all the members know what's going on and have all the information they need.

2. Facilitate group processes—As the group's leader you're always responsible to facilitate the various group processes, such as general decision making, problem solving, and interpersonal communications. Think of yourself as a "process consultant." Your ongoing job is to enable the group's functional mechanics. Whether the members ask for your advice, you offer suggestions, or you silently take care of matters behind the scenes, your responsibility is to help the group succeed by "greasing the skids." Of course you aren't the only group member who facilitates the group's processes, but you are accountable for making sure these operations are attended to and proceed in an effective manner.

3. Model and cheerlead—As long as you are the small group leader, you continue to serve as a model and cheerleader for the other group members. Your attitudes and actions are important to maintaining the group's pace and atmosphere. I'm not talking about being a phony—acting as if everything is okay even when things are falling apart in your life. On the contrary, as a group member you must be real with your emotions, struggles, joys, and attitudes. As the leader you are expected to embody appropriate attitudes and actions. The members look to you to see what you're thinking or how you approach a group situation. How you talk about the group to the members—your upbeat encouraging words—contributes more than you realize to how they in turn view the group. Your positive approach nurtures positive attitudes. Members feel good about the group when you express your satisfaction. When the group is struggling with a difficult situation or problem, how you act and what you say makes a big difference. Your modeling and cheerleading responsibilities never go away.

4. Lead formative evaluation—As we discussed in chapter 6, formative evaluation is a constructive tool you need to use periodically to ensure the group's ongoing health and vitality. This assessment activity remains important even during the group's mature phase. In fact, the need for ongoing evaluation is perhaps more acute among mature groups. Why? Because mature groups can easily slip into deadly routine and complacency without even knowing it. Correctly applied formative evaluation is one means to avoid this undesirable condition. So, coming up in the section titled, "Having Fun?" (page 102) we'll take a closer look at some specifics associated with doing formative evaluation during the group's mature phase.

5. Continue representing the group to ministry leaders—In some cases an individual small group exists or operates within a church's overall small groups ministry. If this describes your situation, then you retain the responsibility to represent your group's interests to the ministry leaders and, in return, the ministry leaders' wishes back to the group. This liaison function plays an especially important role in churches with "high supervision" and "high structure"small group ministries. (see page 49 in *How to Build a Small Groups Ministry*)

TAKING IN THE SIGHTS

Most travelers know where they are going before they set out. When my family and I went to Israel, we knew which countries we would visit (Jordan, Israel, and Egypt) and even our specific day-to-day itinerary. Little was left to chance. The trip had a purpose and was organized to accomplish the planned travel schedule and take in all the desired sights. We made a few adjustments along the way—flexibility is important—but for the most part we did as we had planned.

Successful groups have a central, defined purpose and then are organized and function so as to achieve the stated purpose and its related goals. Sounds simple enough. Yet, it's easy for your group to start well but inadvertently become sidetracked and begin wandering about. Losing your direction results from failing to stay focused on the group's purpose and goals. Remember, every group needs to clearly define why it exists and what it hopes to accomplish. Once done, these specifics serve to direct what you do together as a group.

Some small group advocates suggest there are "generic" or common elements that serve as a purpose and goals for all groups nurtured by local churches. For example, Richard Peace and Thomas Corrigan in *Learning To Care* develop a very good small group model, which includes six basic elements to include in groups seeking to nurture Christian community. Here are the six they suggest:

1. *Care*—The small group as a caring community
2. *Learn*—The small group as a study center
3. *Worship*—The small group as a sanctuary
4. *Enable*—The small group as a training center
5. *Serve*—The small group as a mission center
6. *Outreach*—The small group as a message center

Including all these elements in your group is a lofty but difficult task. Dividing your time and accomplishing the ideals contained in each element requires massive effort on both your and the group's part. If you pull it off, you and the group members deserve high praise. But in my experience few groups are able to embrace all the areas successfully. Most small groups adopting this six-element strategy end up doing several very well, dabbling at several more, and totally neglecting one or two (and usually feel guilty about it). Even Peace and Corrigan are quick to point out that a group isn't likely to operate at the same level or with the same success in all six areas.

Having your group become a center for Christian community is a worthwhile goal. Utilizing Peace and Corrigan's model to do this is a workable option. However, *all* groups needn't fit into this grand design. It's perfectly okay for some groups to pursue a lesser or more limited focus. Limiting your group's purpose and then doing whatever you choose to do well helps reduce the potential frustration. My best advice is to stay focused. Know what you're trying to do and then do it. It's much better to select a more limited group purpose and succeed than to become disconcerted over attempting to do too much. After all, there is more than one type of group, a subject we explore in more depth in chapter 10.

"Taking in the sights" has another application for you as the group's leader. It's important to invest some time in observing what is going on within your group: noting the members' words and behaviors and attempting to discern what they mean. Doing so gives you valuable insight into your members as people, provides clues on how to better serve as their leader, and offers hints on what you might need to do to shore up weak group processes. Unlike formative evaluation, which involves all the group members, the process I'm talking about now is an observational skill you need to develop as a group leader.

When the group's purpose is clear, the format and agenda are established, the members are committed, and the leader is competent, it seems logical that the group should succeed. However, groups do not always follow such a logical, predictable progression. Even in church-related small groups emotionally charged issues, such as harsh attitudes, petty squabbles, extraneous issues, rude behavior, gossip, and indifference, impede group development and growth. People are people, even if they are Christians.

We are always on thin ice in our attempts to associate motives, attitudes, feelings, and so on, with behavior. Nevertheless, your leadership role includes the ability to "read" your group members. I'm not suggesting you become an amateur psychologist and read into everything the members say and do. I am, however, suggesting you become a student of your members. Watch how they act, see what makes them happy or irritated, listen to how they talk about themselves and others, determine how frequently they verbally participate in the group discussions and decision making, and observe how they react to stressful situations. In short, get to know the group members.

Covering all the observational skills useful in getting to know your members is a topic too large for us to fully develop in this brief chapter. Nevertheless, here are five key things to watch for that will provide you with a great deal of useful information about your specific group members.

1. Listen to what each member is saying about the group in general—his or her opinion of the group's activities, members, and purpose. How they talk about the group is a good clue to how they think and feel about being in the group.

2. Watch to see how members participate in group activities. Some members over-participate (dominate) while others may under-participate (withdraw). Yet, don't expect everyone to be involved at the same level. A person's personality greatly influences his or her participation level.

3. Observe how members interact with the other members. Are their words and actions focused on themselves or on other members? How members treat one another is vital to a group's overall success or failure.

4. Note how group members talk about themselves. Do they put themselves down or perhaps overrate themselves? A person with good self-acceptance is able to honestly evaluate his/her attitudes and actions without becoming remorseful or despondent. How a person talks about himself or herself is a good clue to his or her effective participation as a group member.

5. Consider attendance patterns. Members who are absent frequently, habitually arrive late, or routinely leave early may be silently saying something about the group and their own participation. A member's attendance usually, but not always, indicates how he/she feels about being in the group.

Once you obtain a fairly good grasp of what makes each member "tick," use this knowledge to serve needs, to encourage ongoing participation, and to give you a clue when something is wrong. One word of caution, however. Resist branding your members as people who always think or act in a certain way and then expect them to follow suit every time. People are predictable, but at the same time unpredictable. Your goal is to understand the group members, not prejudge them.

When you notice a member demonstrating unusual or atypical behavior the best strategy to interpret the behavior is to ask him or her what's going on. Mustering all your tact, being thoughtful, and choosing your words carefully, inquire if something is on his or her mind or bothering him or her. Offer any assistance you can provide. If it's something outside of your ability to help, be quick to assist him or her in finding the appropriate resolution. Often a person's group participation is affected by situations or relationships outside the group.

Don't be surprised if on occasion you misread the signs. It happens. You think something is wrong but after talking with the member you find out nothing is amiss; it was a temporary problem or you simply misread the indicators. In most cases, even when you are wrong, the member usually appreciates your sensitivity to his or her situation. Just don't overdo it. Some leaders look for problems in every word or action. Falling into this trap can cause you and the group members a lot of discomfort and even grief. Finding the right balance is difficult, but doable with God's help!

ENJOYING THE SCENERY

Living in Oregon for eighteen years, I became accustomed to the beautiful scenery, especially on the coast. On many occasions I recall trips to the coast where I was awed by God's creative genius. The subtle benefits derived from such beauty are still with me today.

As the group's leader, or tour guide, it's your privilege to help the group members identify and acknowledge the benefits they derive from being in the group. By the time the group is in its adult stage, the benefits should be fairly obvious. But don't leave it to chance; take definite steps to help your members identify and celebrate their benefits from being in the group.

Whether through casual conversation or a formal process like formative evaluation, the method of identifying benefits takes second place to the basic need of simply doing it. Any method you think is appropriate for your group is acceptable.

To assist you in helping your group identify the benefits they acquire from group membership, here are some examples of the potential group benefits your members may experience:

- *Mutual care*—The group provides the opportunity for the members to both receive and give care. Members offer and accept practical help in dealing with day-to-day life.
- *Identification*—Everyone wants to belong. The group provides a context where the members can feel like they are needed and important.
- *Expanded thinking and understanding*—Group membership affords the chance to learn new information, explore alternatives, solve problems, and acquire new insights.
- *Needs met*—Group members benefit from having others to turn to in a time of personal, family, or spiritual need. "Bearing one another's burdens" is realized in many groups.
- *Fun*—Life is more pleasurable when you have like-minded individuals with whom to relax and recreate (play). Group membership affords this opportunity.
- *Growth in Christ*—Spiritual maturity is greatly facilitated in a group context and the relationships it provides. The group is a practical lab for Christians to help one another in their individual and mutual spiritual journeys.
- *Servanthood*—Whether leading the group or participating as a group member in a service project, group membership provides a chance for Christian service.

Your group's "scenery" or benefits are very much affected by the group's *cohesiveness*. Cohesiveness is a term widely used in talking about group dynamics. It refers to the overall attraction group members have for one another and the way in which they "stick together." The term describes how members share a mutual sense of belonging and are dedicated to the group's well-being. Indirectly, group cohesion refers to morale, teamwork, or "group spirit." While not always easy to define, it's fairly easy to determine when a group isn't cohesive.

The amount of cohesion directly affects the benefits members experience from being in the group. Consequently, in order for you to promote or enhance the group's cohesiveness and generate potential ongoing benefits for the members, let me share with you some key ideas about cohesion in your group.

- Group cohesion stems from two basic sources: the natural chemistry that exists among the members and the concerted effort you and the members invest in making the group a group. There simply is no way you can make certain the group members all "fit" together. But you and the members can work at building relationships and forging strong bonds.
- A group's cohesion begins to develop starting with the very first meeting. Everything I've shared with you up to this point makes an important contribution. In fact, I'm convinced that group cohesiveness isn't ever fully completed; it's an ongoing, constantly developing, hopefully always improving dynamic.
- The longer a group remains together, the more likely its cohesiveness is to become stronger. While not always true, it makes perfect sense for time to draw the members closer to one another. The more time you and I spend with each other, the greater the likelihood we will remain together and adopt one another's ideas, opinions, attitudes, and even behaviors.
- The degree to which the members' needs are being met by participation in the group directly influences its cohesiveness. If the members view the group as important and meaningful in their lives, they seek to remain in the group and identify with the other members. Group membership and size play important roles. People with similar backgrounds, opinions, age, and other factors more quickly develop cohesiveness, as long as the number of group members, or group size, doesn't preclude meeting individual needs.
- Group norms and cohesiveness are related. Mutual and voluntary compliance with the behavioral and attitudinal expectations causes the members to accept one another more quickly, which in turn contributes to building cohesiveness. Conversely, if norms aren't established or one or more individuals consistently violate the group's "rules," then cohesiveness is retarded and may even be diminished.
- A strongly cohesive group exercises considerable influence

over its members. In addition to the stated group norms, members in cohesive groups are more willing to do what it takes to help their fellow members. Sharing resources—time, abilities, possessions, or finances—becomes prevalent and even expected. Group members begin to depend upon one another, and in my opinion this is good.

- Lastly, group cohesiveness greatly influences the group's purpose, activities, and results. Cohesive groups are highly likely to achieve their stated purpose, enjoy productive activities, and accomplish what they set out to achieve. Regardless of the type of group, cohesion among the members greatly influences the members' satisfaction with the group, and this in turn is manifested in the group's productivity.

So, as you quickly discerned from reading the previous points, group cohesiveness is an important issue in helping your group become a group. For the leader it is a constant concern that needs to occupy your interest and efforts. But how do you know what level of cohesiveness exists within your group? There is no perfect measurement tool, but there are some indicators that can give you some good clues. In the next section we turn our attention to how you can discern these indicators. It's time to do another formative evaluation with your group members.

HAVING FUN?

I remember the tour guide asking my son if he was having fun. What he really wanted to know was how things were going, if the trip was meeting my son's expectations. The guide was seeking information. He was looking for feedback in order to make any needed adjustments so the travelers, in this case my son, would remain satisfied. It was a smart move. I paid attention and took mental notes.

Conducting a formative evaluation at some point in the group's mature stage is strongly encouraged. Remember, formative evaluation is a formal opportunity to get feedback on how the group is doing while there is still time to make any needed adjustments. Such periodic evaluations provide you with an ongoing appraisal of the group's relationships, activities, and goal achievement.

In addition to helping you make in-course corrections, there are two other significant advantages involved with ongoing evaluations. First, formative evaluations involve the members in the group-development process. People do not want to be passive. They prefer being involved; they want to express themselves and be heard. Allowing such expression promotes collaborative processes and strengthens the group's cohesiveness.

Second, formative evaluation encourages the group members to explore their feelings, attitudes, and experiences. By asking the participants to think about their group participation and express themselves, you provide the opportunity to correct any mis-understandings, revise ineffective practices, improve communication, and in general make the group experience a better one. Members often find their feelings or opinions are shared; if no one had expressed them, the possibilities for growth and improvement would have been missed.

But wait, there are more advantages. Involving the members in formative evaluation sensitizes them to their own participation as well as the dynamics associated with becoming a real group. It also helps them develop a sense of ownership. Participating in the evaluation encourages the members to take responsibility for the group's ongoing improvement and success. Formative evaluation is "formal" because it is intentional. You plan to do it; you don't just hope it happens. Ongoing evaluations are conducted in many ways. The following suggestions illustrate that there is more than one acceptable approach. Feel free to modify, adapt, or add to these ideas to fit your specific situation.

- Identify specific times you can meet with individual members to ask how things are going. Sometimes one-on-one encounters reveal information the participant may be reluctant to share with all the members. However, if the issue involves all the group members, you may find it necessary to ask permission to bring the subject up to the whole group.
- Plan an informal dinner or dessert. When people are relaxed, ask them how they think the group is going. Allow for both positive and negative reactions.
- Ask each member to select one word that best describes their

opinion of the group thus far. After everyone shares his or her word, go back and explore the words' implications.

- Formulate a simple questionnaire and have the members fill it out at the beginning of one meeting and then discuss the results at the next meeting.

- Ask the members to write a letter to a real or imaginary friend describing the group. Their letters can be written before the next meeting or you may wish to budget time to write the letters during a meeting. Put all the letters in a hat and then have each member draw one and read it. It's your choice whether or not to have the members sign their letters.

- Rather than making formative evaluation an "event," try concluding each session with two or three minutes devoted to evaluating that particular meeting. Ask the members what went well and is a "keeper" and what didn't seem to go very well and perhaps should be avoided in the future. Using this simple strategy on a regular basis not only contributes to the group's overall development, it also provides the members with an opportunity to become more comfortable with and increase their skill in group evaluation.

Formative evaluations can be verbal or written; both options are workable. Written responses are an especially good strategy early in the group's existence when a certain amount of ambiguity is still present. However, written responses remain a valuable option at any time. If a written format is used, be sure to allow enough time for thinking and reflective answers. Likewise, make certain the "instrument" or questionnaire is well thought-out and constructed. Writing a good questionnaire is a skill, one that may require some help and practice.

Most mature groups should be able to handle verbal feedback. You or the group members may be reluctant to try this, but in my experience it works well if approached properly. Acknowledge the fact that you realize there may be some hesitancy in expressing how you and the members feel about the group, but assure the members it is an opportunity to identify both areas for improvement *and* what the group is doing well. Suggest that the group begin by first identifying what they like about the group before turning to areas of needed improvement. As the leader, you set the parameters for what you want to hear from each person. For example, encourage "I" statements, keep comments to three or four sentences, remind members that nothing is to be repeated outside the group, and so on. You want the members to feel safe in expressing themselves.

Start by asking, "Who will go first?" You may have to ask again and encourage someone to start. But once the sharing begins it normally builds until everyone feels comfortable adding his or her comments and ideas. It's also a good idea to state specific time limits for general discussion before turning to identifying the action steps needed to implement the expressed suggestions or concerns. Likewise, you may find it helpful to have someone jot down notes to keep track of what is said. Written notes also are useful to review your progress at some point later on.

As previously noted in chapter 6, a formative evaluation can include feedback on various group dimensions: administrative details, format, agenda, relationships, or leadership. At this point, as a mature group, everything should be open to evaluation. However, consider focusing the present formative evaluation on assessing the group's cohesiveness. Whether you elect to utilize written responses or conduct an open discussion, here are some examples of open-ended questions you may find useful in exploring the group's cohesion.

- Why do you feel needed as a group member? If you don't feel needed, why not?
- What is the best thing about being in this group?
- How would you describe the relationships among the group members?
- When do you think the group is the most effective: during the meetings or outside the meetings? Why?
- If you were asked to name the group's greatest strength, what would you say?
- How do you feel about the group eventually ending?
- What is your thinking about how the group "cares" for you and the other members?

Allow me one final thought about formative evaluations before we conclude this chapter. Doing a formative evaluation during the group's mature stage is a wise choice. However, you may find the choice is forced upon you by a group "mid-life crisis." It is not uncommon for a group to experience a "flat tire" or "bump in the road" at this point in its existence. Even when everything seems fine, calamity can strike.

Mature groups may experience a challenging crisis when a member or members leave the group, an emergency confronts a member or his or her family, familiar patterns or activities are no longer possible, you as the leader must step aside for whatever reason, the group grows to an unmanageable size, or something dramatic happens in your church or community. In such cases, formative evaluation becomes a valuable tool to help the group assess the situation and formulate an appropriate response. When this occurs, the focus becomes the issue or crisis rather than the group's development. Dealing with such instances often causes the group to rally around one another and ends up producing an even more cohesive group in the long run.

Congratulations, you've completed another chapter. Now you should have a fairly good feel for the characteristics associated with a mature group. Don't despair if your group doesn't match perfectly with everything I presented in these past few pages; few groups do. It's perfectly normal for your group to do well in some areas and not so well in others. The goal is to help your group become a fully functioning group, not merely to conform to some set of expectations.

TAKING ACTION

1. What excites you most about leading and participating in a mature group?

2. Look over the five things you must continue doing during the group's mature phase. Which one do you need the most help with? What can you do to acquire the necessary assistance?

3. Describe your plan to help the members stay focused on the group's purpose and goals.

4. How do you expect to enhance your group's cohesiveness?

5. Imagine it's time for another formative evaluation. What did you learn previously about formative evaluation that you want to include this time around?

CHAPTER EIGHT

Heading Home

The lives of good people are brightly lit streets;
the lives of the wicked are dark alleys.
Proverbs 13:9, *The Message*

E VERY trip eventually concludes. The familiar phrase "All good
things must end" is absolutely true. I recall the final days of my
family's trip to Israel. After almost two weeks it was coming to an
end. We wanted to go shopping one last time in the Old City, visit the
Western Wall again, and eat one last time at McDonalds (classic
Jewish food). Our tour guide did everything he could to honor my
family's and the other tour participants' wishes. He knew these final
activities were important to our forming positive and lasting impressions about the whole trip.

Mature, successful small groups eventually must deal with ending, with drawing the group to a close. Too often, unfortunately, this
final process lacks order and direction. Unless the leader and members plan an orderly finish, it's easy for individual members to
slowly stop coming and drift away until total attendance becomes so
low the remaining members agree not to meet any longer. A slow
disintegration and ultimate demise isn't an ideal picture of a group's
conclusion. The final stage in a group's life cycle provides an excellent opportunity to end with style, reinforce the members' positive
experiences, and set the tone for a continuing groups ministry.

In this chapter we consider what it takes to help your group to
end on an "up beat," to conclude with style and grace. Helping your
group prepare for and accept the group's termination is just as
important as your original efforts to get the group started. Your

group needs to end as well as it began. Leaving all this to chance isn't acceptable.

HEADING BACK

Returning home isn't as glamorous or exciting as first setting out on a trip, but it's just as important. Arriving back home safe and sound after having a good time demands as much attention as preparing to depart. At the end of our trip to Israel, our tour guide didn't just wave good-by and wish us luck in finding our way back to the United States. The return trip also was planned and all the arrangements made. His job wasn't over until we returned safely.

At some point your group enters its final stage: Phase Five — old age and demise (reforming). It may not sound like a glamorous period, but these final five to six sessions are extremely important. The group has been together now for nearly a year, or some other amount of time stipulated in the group's covenant, and is nearing its conclusion. Celebrating struggles and successes is vital, as is dealing with the "grief process" effective groups may experience. Ending the group on a positive note and paving the way for the members' future involvement in groups is important. The group members may wish to re-covenant and continue on or elect to join a new, different group.

You know your group is in its last life-cycle stage when you detect one or more of the following conditions, or perhaps, something unique to your group that's not listed here:

- The stated time period (weeks, months, years) for ending your group is approaching.
- Members attend sporadically and less than half are in attendance at any given meeting.
- Enthusiasm has waned and boredom has set in.
- For tasked-oriented groups, the task is finished or nearly finished.
- A majority of the members express the desire to stop meeting.
- Members' external commitments or other ministries conflict with group participation.
- The topic or issue motivating the content-oriented group is exhausted.

■ The group leader leaves for some reason and no one is willing to assume the position.

Except for the last reason, all of the above conditions are fairly obvious clues you need to do something. However, I don't recommend waiting until the group is falling apart before you take action. Ideally, you are prepared from the very beginning to think about, plan, and discuss with key group members what is involved in bringing the group to a healthy conclusion.

For discussion's sake, let's assume your group's covenant stipulated the group would meet for one year. This means that your concluding date is definable and you know how much time is remaining. Under these circumstances, the group's final life-cycle phase is also determined—the final five or six meetings (but this may be somewhat different in your particular case). Knowing this information gives you the opportunity to take pro-active steps rather than waiting for various clues to indicate it's a good time to begin closing down.

Be prepared: your leadership role needs to change during this final phase. Once again, just as in the beginning, your task becomes more directive. You need to quietly assert your leadership in order to assist the group in its final meetings. Usually the group's dependency on you increases back to earlier levels because they need or want your help. Groups normally want to end on an orderly and positive note.

During this final phase, your job as the group leader is to ensure that the following five basic objectives are accomplished (you may identify others that are appropriate to your specific situation):

1. Help the group members understand and prepare for ending the group.
2. Facilitate reflection and celebration.
3. Conduct a summative evaluation.
4. Assist group members in finding a new group or re-covenanting.
5. Wrap up any last administrative requirements.

Let's consider each of these responsibilities more carefully.

WRAPPING UP THE TOUR

The final meetings arrive before you know it. What you do and how it's done during these last meetings is critical. As I've already said, ending well is just as important as beginning well. Doing so involves accomplishing a great deal, but includes nothing you can't handle. Let's turn our attention to the specifics.

Help the group members understand and prepare for ending the group. Too often, groups begin without considering what it takes to end. Hopefully, this isn't the case with your group. You should have dealt with this issue previously during the time the group formulated its covenant. If you did, it ought to pay off at this point in the group's life. If you didn't, it's imperative you deal with the issue now. Failure to do so may mean misunderstandings and perhaps even hurt feelings. The group members need to understand the what and why connected with the group ending.

Setting a proper tone for concluding involves reviewing the group's purposes, explaining options, stating the timetable, discussing the group's successes (and maybe its failures), and then facilitating the actual process. But these are the objective elements. What you say is secondary to your attitude and how you communicate the information. If you are upbeat about the group concluding it goes a long way in helping the members understand and accept the idea. Conversely, a negative tone or attitude can affect the group adversely. So, as you can imagine, your words and demeanor make a big difference in the dynamics associated with the group's final phase. Stay positive!

You'll find not every member in your group feels the same about ending the group. Some will express disappointment, even remorse. Others may have an opposite reaction. I remember being in several groups where I and others felt elated over disbanding; we literally looked forward to it. Every group isn't a winner. Nonetheless, pro or con, the members need to understand and be prepared for what is involved in the group ceasing to meet.

About five or six weeks before the last scheduled meeting you need to briefly review for all the members what takes place during the final sessions. Feel free to come up with your own, but here is a workable schedule:

- *Three weeks from last meeting*—Review possible alternatives for the future (re-covenant and continue on or new groups); the last formal meeting with the normal format and agenda.
- *Two weeks from last meeting*—Reflection and celebration (the whole meeting; be sure to tell them to come prepared to share what they view as the group's and their own personal highlights).
- *Next to last meeting*—Summative evaluation and, if appropriate, decide about the group's future.
- *Last meeting*—Review the evaluation results, re-covenant, or "going-away" or "new-life" party.

Be sure the group members understand that just because this particular group is perhaps concluding they need not sever any current relationships. They may be in a different group next year, but certainly they can retain and enjoy any friendships they made in the present group. Being in a new group provides the opportunity to make and develop additional friendships, and does not require them to forsake established bonds.

Facilitate reflection and celebration—Have you ever been in a group that just stopped meeting? The members decided to call it quits and spent no time reflecting or celebrating the group's life. Little was said; they just quietly went away. In my opinion these groups miss the opportunity to celebrate God's provision and goodness. Don't let this happen to your group.

I recommend you set aside and dedicate a whole meeting to reflection and celebration. The aim is to recall positive individual and corporate events, praise significant contributions, laugh together over humorous occurrences, identify positive benefits from being in the group, thank the Lord for the opportunity to spend the time together, and in general affirm one another as fellow group members. Any and all subjects are acceptable as long as they assist the group members to revel in their group experience. A festive mood should prevail.

Keep it positive, but I feel strongly about also allowing group members to express any "grief" they have over the group concluding. It's perfectly natural for some or all of the member's to feel sad about departing and want to express themselves. The same goes for any negative feelings about their group experience. Providing an opportunity to discuss any regrets or disappointments that may exist is healthy, as long as you don't allow it to degenerate into a gripe session. Remember, stay positive!

Celebrating about and with your group is so important, and so little is said about it, that chapter 9 is dedicated to exploring this topic in much more detail.

Conduct a summative evaluation—What, evaluate again? Yep, only this time I'm not talking about formative evaluation. Now you need to focus your attention on summative evaluation. Take this leadership task seriously. Evaluation is a critical element that plays an important part in one or more meetings during your group's final phase.

You may recall, back in chapter 6, I said we would deal with summative evaluation in this chapter. Well, that time has come. Summative evaluation is a *formal* process aimed at making decisions about the overall group experience once it has come to an end. Conducting a summative evaluation means collecting information and feedback from the group members in order to make judgments and decisions about the group's success, merits, benefits, and any needed potential improvements. While a series of formative evaluations is geared toward helping the group members improve the group while they are still meeting, the concluding summative evaluation is aimed at providing systematic insight on how the group measured up in reaching its goals. The bottom line is for the evaluation to help you as the leader know whether or not the group accomplished its purpose and fulfilled the members' expectations. In addition, if your church has an overall small groups ministry structure, the evaluation is used to determine if the group achieved whatever was expected by the ministry leadership.

Summative evaluation isn't fault finding. Rather, it is an opportunity to closely examine what went on during the time the group met together. You would be wise to approach the process from an open, curious, and somewhat detached perspective. Doing so helps you and the group members examine your experience from an objective point of view. Identifying what went well and what could be improved, and why, can be accomplished without becoming fixated on trying to point fingers or blame someone for any undesirable outcomes. In fact, I recommend that you steer the group away from protracted attempts to analyze negative circumstances. Oh sure, you need to allow the members to express any negative feelings, but do so in the most positive manner possible. You don't want your summative evaluation to degenerate into a negative experience at this point in the group's life.

As you think about, plan, and then do your summative evaluation, consider three goals to guide your efforts:

1. *Personal evaluation* — Groups are composed of individual members. The evaluation should provide them with an opportunity for personal self-evaluation. This is a private, no-one-else-needs-to-know, confidential process. Only the individual member knows how he or she rates his or her own group participation. Emphasis is placed on personal reflection about his or her experience, participation, and group contributions.

2. *Group evaluation* — This, of course, is the summative evaluation's main thrust; the focus is on how the group did as a group. Did the group sustain its purpose and reach its goals? In addition, the group members are asked to assess outcomes in the following areas:

    a. Details: The suitability of the day, time, and place(s) the group met.
    b. Format and agenda: What the group did at its meetings and how it organized its time.
    c. Relationships: How members accepted, communicated with, and cared for one another.
    d. Leadership: How shared leadership developed and functioned, plus your performance as the group's designated leader (don't fret; view it as an opportunity to learn and grow).

3. *New directions* — Your summative evaluation is an ideal time to secure recommendations about what can be done in the future or what to pursue the next time around if the group is remaining together. The idea is to identify good

practices to keep as they are, methods or patterns that didn't
work and need to be abandoned, and elements that simply
require some minor adjustments but are worth retaining.

Summative evaluation is a big topic and so essential that our
next major section "One Last Look" deals with evaluation "how-
to's" in more detail. But for now, let's finish examining the other
final phase objectives you need to pursue.

***Assist group members in finding a new group or re-covenanting
and continuing on.*** Depending on your situation, you may have two
options when the time comes for your group to conclude. First,
disband and encourage the members to join new groups. This first
option is a normal course of action if your church has an ongoing
small groups ministry that rotates membership on a recurring cycle.
Several churches I participated in, and two I helped start, had group
ministries where everyone "upset the fruit basket" and formed new
groups on a yearly basis. Our groups began in September in conjunction with the new school year and wrapped up in July. We took the
month of August off—a practical decision to allow for vacations and
so forth. Everyone understood the groups cycle and planned accordingly.

Even if your church doesn't have a groups ministry structure, you
and the group members may choose to discontinue meeting. If this
occurs, be sure to encourage the members to find and join new groups.
In addition, you might want to inquire and see if a few members wish
to stick together, invite some new people, and start a new group. This
alternative is equivalent to starting over. You'll need to "go back" and
start from the very beginning in developing the new group.

The second option is to re-covenant and continue meeting. With
this option, the group members decide to remain together and continue functioning as a group. This involves the group reviewing its
covenant—making any additions, corrections, or adjustments the
group deems necessary—and continuing on for another designated
period of time. This second option is a logical choice for many
groups. Consequently, I include a whole section on the topic to conclude this chapter ("Another Trip?").

Whichever option your group pursues, as the group leader you
are responsible to make sure it happens. Do everything within your

power to provide as much assistance as possible. Find out any available information and share it with your group members. Keep them informed. If they have further questions, track down the necessary answers. In short, during the group's final phase it's up to you to set the pace and help the group end well.

Wrap up any last administrative requirements. Most group members don't get involved with this last aspect. However, as the leader you may find it necessary to accomplish certain administrative details your church or organization requires. Final reports, evaluation summaries, or attending a leadership debriefing session are all examples of what I'm talking about. It may be your final opportunity to share what you've learned about your group or groups in general which may be useful to the church leadership. Here again, to repeat myself, stay positive—even if you have negative feelings or information to share.

While it is not normally required, I suggest you write simple thank-you notes to group members. Express your appreciation for their being in the group, thank them for any effort they expended on the group's behalf, and either encourage them to find a new group or tell them how excited you are about the group continuing on. Keep it brief and jovial.

ONE LAST LOOK

A few paragraphs ago I introduced you to the concept of summative evaluation. Now we need to turn our attention to the practical steps required to conduct a summative evaluation for your group. My forthcoming recommendations are just that, recommendations. Feel totally free to make any adjustments to my suggestions you think would better fit and serve your group.

The first question that comes to mind is "When do you do the summative evaluation?" In my experience the best time is the meeting immediately following the one dedicated to reflection and celebration, normally the next-to-last meeting. By this time all the members have had an opportunity to think about their experiences in the group and should be ready to provide some constructive feedback. Besides, if you follow the proposed schedule I outlined previously, the members already are expecting the summative evaluation to take place on the next-to-last meeting.

Please note, evaluation language is important. The words and phrases you use during this process can either facilitate a positive evaluation experience or turn it into a free-for-all with distasteful repercussions. My warning may sound a bit harsh, but for whatever reasons, we as humans frequently react negatively to words. For instance, I find asking, "What are one or two areas needing improvement?" far more neutral and helpful than to ask, "What didn't you like about the group?" or "What problems did we encounter during our time together?" Both latter examples tend to sound derogatory and, consequently, usually generate both derisive attitudes and responses. So, pick your words carefully. Attempt to use language that is as neutral as possible. If you do err in your selection, it's far better to make a mistake by using language that sounds too positive.

Numerous methods are available when it comes to conducting a summative evaluation. Don't worry about finding the perfect way; there isn't one. What you need to do is find a method you feel comfortable with, something that also fits your type of group, its purposes, and its goals. Having said this, let me briefly summarize some workable strategies for you to consider. If something catches your attention and you think you might like to use it, you'll need to go to the library or ask your pastor or a friend how to fully develop and use the method (space doesn't permit me to go into lengthy detail). Furthermore, you're free to mix and match methods as you see fit.

Nearly all evaluation methods I am familiar with and that are suitable for your group's summative evaluation fit in two fundamental categories:

1. Questionnaires—Paper and pencil "instruments" the group members are asked to fill out. This is a popular method but it requires some expertise to use it correctly. The three most common types are:

- Sentence completion: A "stem" begins a statement that the respondent then completes. "The group helped me to . . ."
- Open-ended questions: The most common and most easily abused because the questions often are abstract, long, can be answered yes or no, and/or ask more than one question. Example of a poor question: Did everyone get a chance to participate and share their inner feelings? Example of a good question: What did you appreciate most about being in this group?

- Rating scales: Statements or issues are rated on some kind of numerical scale. "On a scale from 1 to 10, with 10 being the highest, rate how you think the group did in achieving its stated purpose."

If you want to use one or more questionnaire methods you'll need to think ahead and allow yourself enough time to plan, develop, and reproduce your questionnaire. When the time comes, pass out a copy to every group member. If necessary, explain how to fill out the sheet, and then allow group members adequate time to think and respond. Once they are finished you have two choices: collect the questionnaires and take them home to compile the results, or take the time right in the meeting to summarize the findings. Both choices are acceptable. It depends on how much time you have and what else you plan to do at that particular meeting. My personal preference is to take the questionnaires home and produce a written summary I could hand out to everyone at the last meeting.

If you provide a questionnaire for the members to evaluate their personal involvement in the group, don't collect these instruments. After filling them out, the members should keep them for their own reference. You can either budget time for them to complete the forms during the evaluation meeting or have them fill out the questionnaire at home. I prefer to have them do it during the meeting as a part of the whole evaluation process.

Developing a good questionnaire is a skill anyone can learn with a little time and practice. There are several questionnaire examples in *How to Build a Small Groups Ministry* (see Recommended Resource List).

2. Discussions—Some group leaders prefer using group discussion to conduct their evaluation. Let me warn you against selecting a discussion method just because it seems easy to use. A good evaluation discussion takes as much time and effort to prepare and use as any other method. Here are the two most common discussion approaches and their applications:

- Open discussion: Introduce the purpose, set any procedural boundaries, and then let the discussion flow as it may. This option can be deceptive. You would be wise to monitor the time and ensure all the information you need is secured. This may mean bringing up any questions which go unasked.

■ Structured discussion: This option is like using a road map. You plan a series of questions that guide the discussion and allow you to obtain the information you're seeking. You ask each question out loud and then permit the members to respond while you take notes.

If you choose to use discussion as your evaluation method, it's wise for you to set some ground rules or procedural boundaries before beginning. Here are five basic guidelines I recommend (add to the list any additional suggestions you want to include) :

1. Limit the time a person can speak (two paragraphs, two minutes, and so on) about any one issue before allowing someone else to speak or ask questions.
2. Only "I" messages are permitted; speak only for yourself.
3. Challenging ideas or opinions are acceptable, but verbally attacking people is unacceptable.
4. Deal with one issue at a time.
5. Seek a balance between negative and positive issues.

Evaluation discussions require someone to record the comments. You don't want to lose anything said or good ideas offered. As the leader, you may wish to serve as the recorder if you're using a structured discussion. However, if you utilize an open discussion I recommend you have someone else do it; you need to focus on leading the discussion.

I know several group leaders who prefer to use a short questionnaire first and then follow up with a group discussion. Members are asked to individually fill out the questionnaire and, after everyone is finished, then are asked to verbally share their responses as they together proceed from item to item on the questionnaire. This hybrid method works well for leaders who are skilled at using both questionnaires and discussion.

It's often a good idea to budget some time at your very last meeting to review the evaluation findings with your group. This is especially true if you used some type of questionnaire or rating form. You need to let the members know the results. Briefly present the findings and then allow anyone to comment. In some cases the members may want to spend additional time discussing the findings. This is perfectly okay as long as you watch your time and use it productively. In addition, the findings may suggest you need to take some sort of action. This possibility is especially true if your group is planning on re-covenanting and remaining together as a group. If not, the results are valuable information for you, perhaps may enlighten church leadership, and also may provide some interesting insights for the outgoing group members.

ANOTHER TRIP?

My brother and sister-in-law went on several ocean cruises with my in-laws, my wife's mom and dad. Every time they returned they immediately began talking about the next time. They're hooked. It's an experience they thoroughly enjoy and want to repeat as often as possible.

Strong, cohesive groups often find it very difficult to disband. When the situation dictates they must, it is greatly facilitated by making certain everyone knows about the requirement from the very beginning. However, not all groups must discontinue after a predetermined time period. Your group may have the option to re-covenant and continue meeting together.

Can your group continue on? Here are four criteria to help you decide:

1. The church or organization sponsoring your group, if there is one, agrees to allow your group to re-covenant and continue meeting for another stipulated period of time.
2. A majority of the members wants to keep meeting.
3. The re-covenanting process produces a new covenant that all the members embrace.
4. There is no other obvious reason to prevent the group from remaining together.

Other criteria unique to your situation are possible and demand your and the members' consideration. For example, I know one church that required its groups to limit any ongoing group to only 50 percent of the previous membership. They were concerned about groups becoming ingrown. Are there issues unique to your context that require your attention?

Once the decision is made to continue on, and before proceeding, you and the group members need to address several questions:

- What did the summative evaluation tell us about our group? After putting in the time and effort to do a summative evaluation, it makes sense to incorporate the findings into your plans for the on-going group. The re-covenanting process is a good time to capitalize on this information.
- If there's room, assuming one or two members dropped out at the "break," are new members eligible to join the group during the early phases in the new cycle? There are ramifications in answering this question "yes." Unless everyone already knows any new members joining the group, it becomes necessary to go through steps to help the new members achieve the same "groupness" the other members have already gained.
- When shall we re-covenant? The continuing group needs to take seriously the re-covenanting process, just as it did when you first began meeting. The last meeting of the previously stated time period is a good time to rethink and rework your group covenant.

Continuing on as a group provides the opportunity to invest more time in building relationships with group members you already know. The potential for deep, mutually satisfying, caring relationships greatly increases. However, it's also possible to become a closed group others view as being standoffish and closed. The "C" word often pops up: clique. Cliques aren't necessarily bad unless they project themselves as being superior to others or become so exclusive no one else could ever qualify for membership. I don't have to tell you this isn't acceptable and needs to be avoided. You may find it valuable to limit your group to only two or three years, after which time you go through some type of major overhaul, which may include reconstituting the membership in some fashion.

I frequently encounter what I call "perpetual" or "reconstituted" groups. Such groups exist somewhere between being a new group and functioning as an ongoing group. The group identity continues but the members change. One man I spoke with boasted about his group, which had been meeting for more than ten years. A few quick questions told me the group identity was ten years old, but he and his wife were the only remaining original members. Over the years many members had rotated in and out of the group. In my thinking it's pushing it to contend this was the same group. Rather, I argue it was many groups over a period of time. Each time the majority of members change in a group, the group in effect starts over.

This concludes the final stage, the old age and demise phase, in your group experience. Lord willing, it was as positive a time as when the group first began its journey together. The next chapter deals with your tour celebration — celebrating your "groupness."

TAKING ACTION

1. Jot down a few ideas about concluding the group that you may need to share with all the group members.

2. How do you intend to help the group decide if it will re-covenant and remain together or disband?

3. Outline the key items you hope to accomplish during the group's last four meetings.

4. Describe how you intend to conduct the group's summative evaluation.

CHAPTER NINE

Tour Celebration

The aspirations of good people end in celebration;
the ambitions of bad people crash.
Proverbs 10:28, *The Message*

T WO months after my family and I returned from Israel, we were invited to join all our former traveling partners for a party to celebrate our trip. Everyone came with photographs to share, stories to tell, and an eagerness to see one another again. It was a fun time. We laughed, reminisced, and strengthened the bonds that had developed during our journey. In fact, my family subsequently has become very close to another family who shared the trip with us.

This short chapter focuses our attention on a dimension of group life that is too seldom included in discussions or recommendations about small groups. I'm talking about celebrating your "groupness." After investing so much time and energy in helping your group become a group during the year, or whatever amount of time you spent together, it seems sad not to schedule an opportunity for the members to capitalize on their mutual experience. You need to plan and have a "tour celebration," a party to highlight the good times and benefits you gained together as a group.

Let me suggest just three basic reasons why it is important for you to plan and have a "tour celebration" with your group members:

1. Closure is necessary. Like graduation from high school or college, a concluding party affords an opportunity for the members to emotionally and psychologically bring closure to being in that particular group. This dynamic assists the members in moving on to their next group or paves the way for the group's next cycle if they are going to continue meeting. Either way it places a formal "blessing" on the previous time they invested in group membership and participation.

2. *God deserves credit.* A final party is an excellent chance to celebrate God's blessing on the individual members and on the group as a whole. I'm assuming your group had a spiritual emphasis and sought God's direction during the time you met. If so, it makes perfectly good sense to invest some time in celebrating God's involvement in your group. He was the unseen group member. Besides, God deserves all the attention and praise we can give Him.

3. *It's fun.* I know Christians aren't supposed to have fun, but let's abandon this foolish (and I might add unbiblical) idea and go ahead and do it anyway. What better lasting memory to give your group members as a going-away gift than to wrap up their group experience with a delightful time together. Ending the group on a high note, one that emphasizes the great times you had together, is a fitting and proper finale.

THE TOUR PARTY

We already looked at why a celebration is a grand idea, now let's check out the other details by using the familiar who, what, when, and where. I'll make some suggestions, but I'm sure you can come up with many more ideas specifically suited to your group.

***Who*—**This seems obvious enough. The group members are the ones who most need to celebrate the group experience they had together. However, there are others you may wish to invite and include in your party. Consider extending invitations to the members' families, key church leaders, and perhaps your pastor. Including others, especially family members, helps accentuate the value associated with being a group. I think it's especially important to invite family members. Our children need to see and experience being with other adults who share our spiritual convictions. This influence is depicted in Scripture as an integral part of the Hebrew culture. Children profit from being exposed to adults other than parents or relatives who share the same beliefs and values. However, a word of caution: don't invite so many people that you lose the emphasis on the group and your final celebration.

What—The sky is the limit. Almost any format or party theme is acceptable. Be creative, but don't invest excessive time or money to pull it off. The best bet is to keep it simple. Usually the group members are just happy to get together. A potluck dinner, picnic, or informal evening featuring a fancy or unique dessert are good options. I suggest you do something that gives the people plenty of time just to talk and share stories. Going to a stage play, amusement park, or even a restaurant aren't the best options because the focus isn't the members' "groupness." Here are three good ideas to start you thinking:

1. **Costume party:** Have the members choose a country they think best represents their group experience together. For example, Japan because the group members were polite and courteous to one another or Italy because the members were full of life and talked a lot with their hands. Ask everyone to think up and wear to the party some unusual and creative costume that depicts something about the chosen country. Have a good time trying to guess the meaning of one another's outfits. Decorations and party favors suitable to the country are a nice touch. You may want to combine this idea with the next.

2. **Ethnic dinner:** Let's say everyone in your group likes Mexican food. Ask each member to make (or buy) a favorite dish and bring it along with anything else he or she wishes to provide (napkins, paper plates, or drinks). Share the food and enjoy the fellowship. You may want to consider going to a Mexican (or whatever) restaurant, but only if they have a separate party room they rent or allow you to use.

3. **Pen pals:** Write everyone's name on small pieces of paper you then fold and tape shut. Put the names in a hat and as the members arrive, ask them to pick one but not to open it until told to do so. After everyone has arrived and you're ready to begin, pass out two pieces of writing paper and one envelope to each person. Ask members to open their slips of paper and, using one piece of the writing paper, write a note to the person they picked thanking them for something specific about their group participation. Make sure they put the person's name on the paper and sign the note. When everyone

is finished (allow at least ten to fifteen minutes) collect the notes, mix them up, and then randomly pass them out making certain neither the author nor the addressee receives his or her note. Go around the room and have each member read out loud the note you gave them. After everyone has read a note, tell the members it's time to write one last message . . . to themselves. Ask them to write a note to themselves about one lesson they learned, a good memory, or perhaps something they found out about themselves by being in the group. Tell them to address their envelopes to themselves, put the notes inside the envelopes and seal them, and hand them in to you. Inform them you will mail the notes back to them in six months (make certain you do). Spend the rest of the time enjoying each other's company.

Whatever you plan to do, include plenty of time for the group members to interact with one another. The format and agenda are secondary to helping the members have one last good time together. Just getting together for coffee is the best idea for many groups.

When—Choose an occasion suitable to most members, a day and time that allows the greatest number to attend. With this in mind, I find it works well to plan the party for the last official group meeting before disbanding or beginning the next cycle. The members already are used to meeting at this time and it tends to sidestep reasons for not participating. However, some groups wait and have a "reunion" party several weeks or months after the group has concluded. This option is often a good idea for groups that discontinued meeting but want to maintain some contact with their former group members. One down side to this option: I notice the attendance is usually somewhat or a lot less than ideal. People move on in their lives, and finding a good time to meet becomes harder the longer you wait after the group is officially done. Of course, having a party now and later also is a good choice.

Where—The place really doesn't matter unless your group has developed an attachment to a particular spot, such as the location where you met regularly. I find it best to pick a place that doesn't distract the members. As I mentioned before, theaters, amusement parks, or other public places can turn the focus away from the group celebration. I especially advise against meeting in a restaurant unless you can have your own area separate from all the other customers. Anywhere you plan to meet needs to provide maximum opportunity for the group members to talk and fellowship, prevent outside distractions, and permit the group to get a little "rowdy" if members so desire.

LOOKING AT THE PHOTOGRAPHS

At our Israel tour party, which I mentioned at the beginning of this chapter, we found ourselves looking at the photographs and remembering places we had visited, meaningful events we shared, enjoyable activities, and especially the people who played an important part in our tour. The pictures prompted us to recall people who were significant to the success of our trip. Thinking about the tour guide, translators, street vendors, bus drivers, and of course, each other stimulated rich memories.

Your group may or may not have photos you or another member took during your time together. Either way, it is important to spend some time at your celebration looking at the real or imagined photographs and remembering the events and especially the people. Specifically, you need to facilitate a process whereby the group members have the opportunity and sufficient time to reflect and remember. I've noticed it's easier for most men to remember events, while women tend to remember relationships. Both group elements are important and need examination. Focusing the group's attention on these vital issues can happen many ways.

In the last section, I gave you several ideas about the group celebration's "what," the format or party theme. Regardless of what format you choose, you need to focus on celebrating in three specific areas—events, people, and results. For discussion's sake I separate them into distinct categories. However, in reality they blend together easily. Don't worry about keeping the ideas separated during your celebration party. You'll find the group members jumping around in their thinking and comments anyway.

Events: Routine or special group events should be examined. Encourage the members to identify activities, events, outings, or experiences that they found meaningful. The idea is to recall anything that left a lasting impression and contributed toward the members' betterment. Small routine events or happenings are perfectly acceptable. You'd be surprised what some people find significant. It's not always the big things that leave the most lasting impressions. How you go about doing this is secondary. Simple "around-the-room" sharing works perfectly fine. However, with this element and the next two, I strongly suggest you not urge the members to share unless they want to. Doing so can dampen the party atmosphere. Lord willing, your group members are so excited about the group you have to monitor how much they talk, not worry about getting them to talk.

People: The real glue that held the group together, and perhaps the group's key purpose is the relationships nurtured in the group. This is the "mushy" time when members express their gratitude for one another. Not everyone is good at this venture. Hopefully by now the members feel somewhat comfortable expressing themselves to one another. Simple thank-yous to more emotional comments are admissible. You needn't put any restrictions on the sharing. If appropriate, you also may want to encourage the members to recognize anyone outside the group who was instrumental in helping the group, for example, a pastor, babysitter, neighbor, or church secretary. Writing a thank-you note everyone signs is a nice idea. Even better, call these individuals on the telephone and have several members express their thanks.

Results: Looking back, recognize the overall results or outcomes the group members gained from being in the group. This is the opportunity to sum up the group's total time together, a chance to summarize the best and most significant highlights. Focus in on the group experience, the "groupness" aspects. You want to talk about your mutual "life" together. While personal perspectives are important, and hopefully have been shared by this time, now the attention is turned to the "us," "we," and "our" group dimensions. Lead the members in reflecting on its corporate growth, progress, and overall development. It's a terrific chance to recognize how God assisted the group in becoming a group.

"Looking at the photographs" needs to emphasize the most positive aspects associated with being in the group together. Everyone knows there were some rough spots, but now isn't the time to dwell on those facets. Remember, the goal for having the celebration is to embed positive, affirming memories in the members' thinking. In addition, it is an opportunity to create a springboard into their next group or, if the group is continuing on, the next covenant cycle. Keep it upbeat!

TELLING YOUR FAMILY AND FRIENDS

My brother-in-law and sister-in-law keep trying to get my wife and I to go on a cruise with them. They have enjoyed themselves so much that they're always urging us to join them on their next trip. They are sold and want to sell us on the experience (you'd almost think they work for the cruise line company).

Lord willing, you and your group members had such an outstanding experience together that you are all eager to have others encounter the same benefits. Being in a small group with fellow believers has great potential, hopefully potential your group achieved. But you mustn't keep the group experience a secret. I encourage you to share it with as many people as possible: family members, friends, coworkers, and church members.

There is no limit to the possible ways you can tell others about the joys and benefits associated with group membership. For example, other than one-on-one conversations, which are the best option, here are five ideas to spark your imagination:

1. Brief testimonies in your church newspaper or Sunday morning bulletin—Ask several members to write brief statements about their group experience. Funny stories, poignant moments, unusual occurrences, overall benefits, personal insights, and friendships established are all examples of what to include. Ask them to keep their statements short and to the point. Make arrangement to publish one or two stories each week for two or three weeks. This option works well in smaller churches. Many larger churches don't have room in their worship folder or bulletin. Nevertheless, with enough advance planning, it is quite possible to include one or more statements in your church newsletter. If your church doesn't have a newsletter, consider publishing your own "groups newsletter" or pamphlet, which extols the virtues of group membership and provides specific information on how the reader can participate.

2. Interview one or two members—A terrific idea is to interview one or two group members during a regularly scheduled worship service. A morning service is best because more people are present, but many traditional churches reserve such activities for their evening service. There's something dynamic about hearing a real, live person talk about his or her experience in a small group. Keep the interviews under five minutes. Don't forget to say something about how those listening can become involved in small groups.

3. Have an "information meeting"—Schedule a specific time and invite people to come and learn more about your small group or your church's small group ministry. Having the meeting immediately before or after another regular event (worship service, Sunday school, or mid-week service) usually works well. Make certain to publicize the meeting far enough in advance so everyone knows about it and can attend. I recommend that the informal meeting last no more than thirty or forty-five minutes. Your agenda should include upbeat presentations outlining the small group vision, goals, details, and how to become involved. Some type of handout or brochure the attendees can take with them, including the name and phone number of someone they can contact if they have questions, is a must. Stay within your time limits. Serving refreshments is fine.

4. Create a small groups bulletin board— One church I know implemented a great idea: the staff installed in their church narthex a large bulletin board dedicated to their small groups ministry. All the groups were identified—who, what, when, where, and so on. Maps, brochures, and photographs were strategically included. Coming into the church, a person couldn't miss the board. The display really did an excellent job of highlighting this important ministry. You may not be able to dedicate a whole board to small groups, but you can utilize one for a month or so to "report" on your specific group's success. Look at it as a first opportunity, one that you may get the chance to expand at a later time.

5. Put together a photo scrap book— A novel idea is to take photographs of the group throughout it's time together, including the final celebration, and then compile the photos into an album. It's like a family scrapbook that depicts the group's life. Once finished, place the album in a prominent place so people notice it and are free to look it over. Eventually you might even want to keep it on the coffee table in your home for visiting friends and family to examine. It could potentially stimulate some interesting conversations and the chance to share how much the group meant to you. Who knows, you might even get the chance to recruit some new group members or share the gospel with a nonbeliever. It certainly doesn't hurt to give the idea a try.

LOOKING FORWARD TO THE NEXT TOUR

We weren't home from Israel for more than a few days before my family began to talk about how much they wanted to go back. It was such an enjoyable journey that we found ourselves plotting our return. Oh sure, there were some things we wouldn't want to duplicate, but overall it was a terrific time we definitely want to repeat in the near future.

Hopefully, the majority of your group is eager to continue in group membership—in a new group or by remaining together in the same group. Your tour celebration is a good time to heighten this anticipation.

The final thing you need to do at your celebration is to talk about what comes next. It's the perfect opportunity to set the stage for ongoing group participation. Three basic options are most likely: new groups, the same group continuing on, or no group.

New groups—If the opportunity exists to join a new group, make certain everyone knows the options, details, and specifically what to do next. Offer to provide any needed assistance. Send them off in an approving manner. It's a good time to wish everyone well and thank them for being in your group.

Group continuing on—If your current group previously elected to continue on, now you need to inform them what comes next. Re-covenanting is your first business to consider. Be ready to propose a new schedule and agenda for them to contemplate. It's not likely you can re-covenant at your group celebration, so don't depart until everyone knows when the next meeting occurs and the meeting's intended agenda.

No group—On occasion, no group participation is on the horizon. Whether the members don't want to continue in a group or no opportunity exists (for example, your group elects to disband and there are no other groups to join), the goal is to leave the door open for future participation. Nothing may be available now, but ask those who might be interested in joining a group again in the future to sign a roster you place on the coffee table or kitchen table. You're not promising anything, you simply want to keep them informed if circumstances change.

You may have members who remain silent during this last segment, and that's perfectly okay. You don't want to draw attention to them by asking them to state their intentions. If someone is silent, take note and speak with him or her after the meeting or during the next week. Once in a while you'll encounter members who are squeamish about revealing their future group plans at the party because they aren't sure what they're going to do next, are planning to quit altogether and don't want to dampen the festive mood, or some other reason.

Once the "tour celebration" is complete, you are ready to re-channel your time and energy into the next new group or next group cycle, if your present group is remaining together. But before you restart any group cycle, the next chapter deals with some very useful general information about becoming a group.

TAKING ACTION

1. State in your own words why you think your group deserves and should have a final celebration.

2. Develop a plan for a celebration party you can suggest to the group; don't forget to account for who, what, when, and where.

3. Identify the events, people, and results you think deserve recognition at the group's celebration.

4. List several ways you'd like to tell others about the joys and benefits associated with group membership.

5. What do you plan to do to help set the stage for the group members' ongoing involvement in a group?

CHAPTER TEN
Trip Strategies

Wise men and women are always learning,
always listening for fresh insights.
Proverbs 18:15, *The Message*

I F you read the previous chapters, you already know my family and
I went on a tour to Israel. Did we have any other option; was it
possible to go somewhere else? You bet! We could have gone anywhere in the world (okay, maybe not anywhere). First we decided on
Israel, next we had to determine where in Israel we wanted to visit
and what we wanted to do. We relied heavily on the tour guide to
help plan an engaging itinerary for us and the other tour participants.

Becoming a real group requires that you and the group members
invest time and energy. You could all have spent your time on other
activities, yet you chose to participate in the group. Once you
decided to form a group together, you had to determine your purpose,
goals, format, and agenda. Your options were numerous. More than
one group strategy was possible.

In this final chapter, we examine selected topics, which deal
with groups in general, various options and strategies you need to
know about. This information will increase your understanding about
groups and also may provide some useful insight in helping your
group succeed. It's practical stuff because your group depends on
you to help them become a real group.

MORE THAN ONE DESTINATION

Like tours or trips, groups may have different destinations or reasons
for existing. The options are endless. It all depends on what you're

trying to accomplish. Groups can offer many choices to their members. I'm convinced groups provide the most versatile ministry formats available to the local church. This abundant variety has to start somewhere, have a beginning point. I think we need to return to the definition for small groups that I gave you in the first chapter. By doing so I can set the stage for exploring some of the potential group options. So once again, here is the generic definition I use:

> A small group within the church is a voluntary, intentional gathering of three to twelve people regularly meeting together with the shared goal of mutual Christian edification and fellowship.

Since this definition is our beginning point, it's useful for me to explain it phrase by phrase.

Within the church—The definition, and this whole book, assumes a local church or religious organization is the general context or sponsor for your group. Such groups, unlike most other groups in education or business, have a defined spiritual dimension and purpose. Consequently, they exist and operate under the direction of the Holy Spirit and embrace biblical standards and values.

Voluntary—Potential members cannot be forced to join a small group; they must choose to participate. People need to know and understand, see and experience the value of group membership. Just as salvation cannot be forced on people, group attendance must not be forced.

Intentional gathering—Small groups are intentional, planned events, not random happenings left to chance. Clear purpose and design characterize the types of groups included in our definition. They systematically bring people together for deliberate reasons.

Three to twelve people—Group size is very important! When your group's membership grows beyond twelve people, fifteen at most, it becomes difficult to maintain effective interpersonal relationships and accomplish the group's goals. Sure, larger small groups can work, but the chances of success are reduced. Jesus' group included only twelve people besides Himself. If a group this size was adequate for Jesus, who was God, I suggest we follow His example.

Regularly meeting together—Groups can exist merely on paper and never meet. However, the definition is referring to groups that gather together on a regular and consistent basis. Group meetings are scheduled for a definite time, on an particular day, at a specific place, and for a specified length of time. My current group meets at 6 A.M. on Wednesday mornings at an office for one and a half hours. But any other option suitable to the group is perfectly okay.

With the shared goal—The group's purpose or intent is clearly stated. Members participating in groups understand, accept, and actively promote the mutually shared goals. While many specific goals and objectives may guide a group's existence, three general features are implied by our definition: mutuality, edification, and fellowship. Read on.

Mutuality—The old saying "one for all and all for one" grasps the "mutual" concept included in our small group definition. Every member must assume responsibility for the group's success. Both the leader and members are accountable for group relationships, goals, activities, processes, tasks, and results.

Christian edification—The Greek words for "edify" (*oikodomeo*) and "edification" (*oikodome*) literally mean "to build" or "building up." Add the word "Christian" and the meaning develops the idea of strengthening or reinforcing believers' spiritual lives. So, regardless of a group's specific purpose or activities, everything must focus on building up Christians. The apostle Paul reminds us, "Let all things be done for edification" (1 Corinthians 14:26).

Fellowship—*Koinonia* (fellowship) is the real cement in building successful small groups. Much more than coffee and donuts, biblical fellowship means sharing things in common, communion with one another based on our mutual relationship with Jesus Christ (1 Corinthians 1:9). In 1 John 1:7, we are told that if "we walk in the light" we have fellowship with one another. Small groups provide a key context in which we can actively realize genuine Christian relationships.

The definition we just reviewed is flexible. *There is no one right kind or type of group.* Many different kinds of small groups can fit into the definition. So, let's examine the options.

As I said previously, your group must have a central thrust or *primary focus*, the reason why the group exists—its goals. Numerous options are possible, but my experience has led me to identify four basic kinds of groups, which fit within our definition and reflect diversity in purpose:

1. Relationship-oriented group—The group focuses on being a group. That is, the group's primary purpose is facilitating spiritual and/or social relationships among its members. What the group does is secondary. Emphasis is placed on group identity, relationship dynamics, and the processes necessary to bring these about. Terms such as "growth group," "caring group," "fellowship group," or "covenant group" often are used to describe groups that fit into this classification. Relationship-oriented groups come in different shapes and forms depending on what format, methods, and activities are used.

2. Content-oriented group—Included in this second classification are a variety of Bible study and discussion groups. The main reason for meeting is to study or discuss a biblical passage or topic. Interpersonal relationships are of concern, but most often are merely assumed. Little time is spent on dealing with group dynamics, if any. The primary focus is on the content, ideas, information—the intellectual data.

3. Task-oriented group—These are "doing" or work-centered groups. The primary thrust is to accomplish a defined task, job, or assignment. Consequently, the group's task is its purpose for meeting, the reason for the group's existence. Relationships among the members take a secondary role and usually aren't dealt with unless a problem arises. The group members may not even view themselves as being a group. Most committees and planning groups fit into this category. Likewise, evangelism groups are usually task-oriented.

4. Need-oriented group—Groups in this category focus on a common need and/or interest among the group members. Frequently called support groups or recovery groups, the members meet together for common support and understanding. The group members' attitudes and actions say, "I understand your struggle; I've been there myself." Alcohol recovery, parents of gay children, divorce recovery, or battered women are all examples of need-oriented groups. Some groups in this category require a specially trained leader (such as a counselor, social worker, or pastor).

These four categories aren't rigid and don't necessarily account for every variation. In fact, some churches find it useful to combine several types and produce hybrid groups. For example, one church in

Indiana is entirely structured around ministry teams—relationship-oriented groups that share a specific ministry task: Missions Team, Junior High Ministry Team, Worship Team, and so on. It's a great idea and works well for them.

Keep in mind that no one type of group is ideal or preferred. All serve a purpose and can be effective. Some churches elect to use only one type, such as relationship- or content-oriented groups, and utilize various formats and activities within that group type. Other churches, especially larger churches, offer all four types and even devise new options. It all depends on what needs to be accomplished. Moreover, the types of group selected dictate the dynamics associated with helping the group become a real group. Let me quickly outline a partial list to illustrate what I mean. As the leader you need to remain alert to and address these issues; if you don't they may hinder your group from reaching its potential.

Relationship-oriented group
- Emotionally or spiritually "closed" members resist opening up
- Tendency exists to become merely a social gathering
- An especially needy member turns it into a personal, ongoing therapy group
- A productive format and agenda is difficult to find

Content-oriented group
- People enjoy the content, but not each other
- Needs exist among the members but are not addressed
- Too much material is covered and application is neglected
- Some members don't complete the necessary preparation for each meeting

Task-oriented group
- People issues are forsaken because the focus is solely on the task
- Members don't share the task load on an equal basis
- The task is not completed
- Lack of adequate skills, knowledge, or resources makes it impossible to complete the task

Need-oriented group
- All participants are not accepted equally
- Lack of focus moves the emphasis beyond the group's stated purpose
- Unbalanced participation or domination is caused by overly dependent members
- Leadership is inadequately trained

The issues I listed don't exhaust the possibilities. However, they do highlight some key problems that hinder efforts to become a real group. Your leadership makes a big difference in whether or not these issues, or others unique to your situation, make or break your group.

KNOW THE ROADBLOCKS

Becoming a real group takes time and effort. You know this. Consequently, you also need to know about some potential road-blocks—ineffective group behavior patterns that, if developed, are likely to prevent your group from becoming a real group. Here are seven to watch out for.

The minimum-risk group—A group takes on this mantle when the members are not willing to open up and share on a personal level with one another or if they aren't willing to experience new and different formats, activities, or tasks. For relationship-oriented and need-oriented groups this behavior pattern is deadly because such groups are designed to facilitate relationships. Taking risks with activities or tasks is secondary. Content and or task-oriented groups aren't influenced as severely, but can easily allow the members to "hide" from one another by focusing only on the content or task, totally ignoring even minimally acceptable interpersonal relationship levels.

The minimum-risk group is listed first because it is the most common type of problem. It usually develops when the members fail to discuss and come to a mutual understanding about the group's purpose and goals. In addition, it can occur if the format and agenda don't occasionally stretch the members' comfort zone. But whatever the cause, the minimum-risk group usually fails to explore the more challenging relationship options or activities, which are most useful in helping the individuals develop into a group.

The bull-session group—The bull-session group is a minimum-risk group that uses a discussion format almost exclusively. Their discussions tend to get off track easily, one or two members often dominate, or members share personal ideas and opinions that have few biblical roots. While basically nothing is wrong with a discussion approach, experience shows that when groups slip into this as an exclusive format, it's easy to get stuck in a rut. Before long many members feel the group is unproductive and not accomplishing anything—all talk and no action.

Avoiding the bull-session roadblock is achieved in at least two ways. First, talk about it with the group. Don't be shy; help them see the need to avoid merely talking for talk's sake, sharing ignorance, or wasting time in pointless discussion. Second, explore other meeting formats and methods. Include discussion, but also try some new meeting strategies.

The social-life group—Members in this happy group enjoy one another so much they prefer just to party with one another. Every meeting turns into a social gathering and productivity isn't a concern. Friendships are important, but in this case they eliminate all else. Often no emphasis is placed on deeper spiritual or relational issues. Friendships are shallow and limited to fluffy interaction and involvement. Relationships are normally the "glue" which holds a group together. However, in this instance social interaction is mistaken for meaningful, genuine relationships.

The social-life group emerges when the group lacks a clear purpose or when you as the leader allow it to take place. It is a common occurrence in groups. After all, humans are social beings. Periodic formative evaluation is one method to identify and correct, or should I say re-channel, this tendency. Good meeting planning also helps. You want your group to facilitate strong, honest relationships among the members because doing so provides the basis for becoming a real group.

The holier-than-thou group—Becoming a true group is stymied when the group takes on a hyper-spiritual character and expectations for its members. Reality is avoided because no one wants to admit they have problems or needs. Judgmental attitudes prevent the members from accepting and appreciating one another. The group ends up becoming a "holy huddle" where only the most pious (in their own opinions) are welcome and feel comfortable.

Your leadership style and attitude is the best way to avoid becoming a holier-than-thou group. Most groups falling prey to this dilemma do so because their leader sets the pace. He or she thinks such attitudes and behavior are necessary and required. So, in this case it's very much up to you.

The codependent group—Ineffective groups in this category are marked by members who rely too heavily on one another or depend on the leader to do everything. Too often the leader accepts this role or isn't willing to share the leadership tasks. Healthy inter-personal relationships are lost in the members' desire to please one another. Members find it difficult or impossible to act unless every-one is in total agreement. Concern for one another's feelings and welfare goes to impossible extremes and prevents open and honest evaluation. Or the leader is so dominant that only members who demonstrate high dependence on the leader can survive in the group.

The key to avoiding this pitfall is for each and every member to accept responsibility for the group's purpose, function, and results. All the members need to view their participation as a commitment. It means taking turns planning and leading meetings or segments within a meeting. It also means sharing equally in making various group decisions and participating in open and honest group evalua-tions. But most importantly, it means that you as the leader have to understand and adopt shared leadership and eventually allow the group to take responsibility for itself.

The mini-groups group—This debilitating group roadblock is subtle and often goes unnoticed as a group grows larger. The members begin to divide up among themselves and create sub-groups within the group. These questionable cliques are mani-fested by behavior such as always sitting together, restricting conversation to one another, and "taking sides" against other group members. What happens is the group really becomes several groups within the group.

Many factors can lead to mini-groups within a group. However, the two most common are group size and member composition. As the membership increases, the group eventually gets too large to maintain relationships among all the members, so they begin to divide themselves into sub-groups with other like-minded individuals. This dividing tendency also is provoked when the group members come from two or three distinct social or religious backgrounds. While these divisions are usually unintentional, people feel most comfortable with others like themselves. Unless this tendency is acknowledged and discussed, as alive and well in this roadblock, we all have a propensity to fall victim to divisiveness.

The new-church group — A potential for real conflict. Some groups are so successful they compare their success with what they view as a weak church experience and conclude they need to use the group as a basis for starting a new church. This reaction may be true and correct, but extreme caution is advised.

Spending group time criticizing the church or its leaders is strictly unacceptable in my thinking. Engaging in such behavior is not only unbiblical (Matthew 18:16; 1 Timothy 5:17,19; Hebrews 13:17), it also casts a shadow over the group itself. It's very difficult to build a positive, productive group if you dwell on negativity. If legitimate concerns arise you would be wise to have your group invite the involved party to attend a meeting where you can air your concerns. But in the end, I urge you not to lead a group which facilitates dissension or sedition.

MAKE THE TRIP COUNT

The small university where I formerly served as president sponsored the trip to Israel my family and I hosted. This sponsorship was clearly stated in all advertisements and promotional materials. Little chance existed to miss the point. The tour was planned to benefit both the participant and the school. We wanted the participants to enjoy themselves and consequently think well of the university. Making the trip count resulted in their benefit and increasing our institutional reputation.

The central theme in this book is helping your group become a real group. This "internal" emphasis is foundational. Yet a successful group must also produce "external" benefits. That is, your group not only exists for the members' benefit, but it should also enhance or build a positive reputation for your church or sponsoring organization. Most groups, but certainly not all groups, are linked to a church or organization. Three options are possible.

Local church—Many groups are sponsored by individual churches. Whether an independent congregation or one affiliated with a specific denomination or religious group, churches are the most common context in which the kinds of groups we're talking about in this book are found. Nearly all the groups I've been in were connected with a local church.

Christian organization—Small groups are utilized by many Christian organizations: The Navigators, InterVarsity Fellowship, Campus Crusade for Christ, Promise Keepers, and Bible Study Fellowship, for example. The list is long. In fact, many such organizations depend on small groups as the central method by which they conduct their ministries. For them, being in a group is often required.

The Church—Here I am referring to the "universal" church, the body of Christ, which includes all believers regardless of their religious or denominational identification. Some groups have no specific organizational connection whatsoever, such as the men's group I attended for nearly four years. Lacking an identified church or organizational sponsor, we still were brothers in Christ and shared membership in the body of Christ. We functioned as a group representing Christianity in general.

Second Corinthians 5:20 comes to mind. It says, "We are *ambassadors* for Christ" (emphasis added). Wow, what an important and challenging responsibility we share. Representing Christ is a privilege group members share within the group. Moreover, it is a responsibility they share outside the group; it's their group "reputation." Just like a person, a group has a reputation. I trust your group's reputation conforms to the standard set forth in John 13:35: "This is how everyone will recognize that you are my disciples—when they see the love you have for each other" (MSG).

One additional biblical passage is worth considering. Quoting from *The Message*, Proverbs tells us, "Earn a reputation for living well in God's eyes and in the eyes of the people." Yes, this is an expectation for me as an individual, but it also represents an ideal that should characterize my group and, of course, your group. When it does, it not only enhances the group's reputation, it also reflects well on your sponsoring church or organization or on the body of Christ in general. I'm positive you will see how important it is for your group to "count."

BEYOND YOUR CONTROL

Stand by! Be on the alert! External forces are at work and they can seriously affect your group. No group exists in a vacuum. Things outside the group like community values, church identity, family pressures, and work demands all influence your group members and subsequently the group as a whole. Subtle or glaring external factors can pop up during any phase in your group's life cycle and demand your attention.

Wouldn't it be great if leading a group meant you had complete control of all the dimensions affecting your group? However, you don't. There are influences or factors outside your reach. You may find yourself in a position where your group strategy has to compensate for factors that are beyond your ability to control. Sometimes these external forces are "restrictive"—certain goals and means aren't allowed. You face limits on what you can and cannot do as a group. On the other hand, external dynamics may provide an "expansive" influence. In either case, external forces are likely to influence your group's journey in becoming a real group.

It's impossible for me to identify all the potential external influences that can impact your group or to recommend a response to every possible situation. However, let me give you a little taste of some common external influences you might encounter.

Your church—If your group is sponsored by your church there may be expectations or restrictions you must observe. Here's one extreme example: A church I'm familiar with requires its groups to follow a prescribed format, agenda, and content. Group leaders aren't permitted to deviate from the expected routine. Accepting the responsibility to lead a group also means endorsing the external control the church leaders exercise over all their groups.

Your community—Every community has its values system and social activities. You may think going swimming at the lake is a great idea for a group outing. However, in some southern states in the United States "mixed bathing" (men and women swimming together) is frowned on; Christians don't participate in such an activity. Selecting another outing is your best alternative.

Members' families—Family pressures and expectations often impact group members and, consequently, how the whole group functions. For example, a young couple in one of my groups didn't feel comfortable leaving their newborn son with a babysitter. Instead, they brought the child to our group meetings. It caused some confusion and disruptions at first, but before long the group adjusted and even grew to appreciate having the child in its midst. However, as a rule, bringing babies to the group doesn't work.

Members' work—Members' work schedules can change and interrupt their consistent group participation. The men's group I attended for several years was composed of upper-level business executives who traveled often for their companies. It was fairly common for half of our sixteen members to be absent from our group meetings.

Members' other activities—Group members are busy people who frequently are involved in other important activities. One group I participated in had four members who also sang in the church choir. Their attendance at group meetings became very irregular several times a year when the choir was rehearsing for major musicals our church performed for the community at large. Their loyalties were split. They valued their group membership, but singing in the choir was a big deal to them, and they were forced to choose. Unfortunately, the group came out second.

Rarely can you as a group leader control any of the situations I just described or the ones you'll encounter in your context. In most cases you have to roll with the punches and adjust the best you can. Getting frustrated or badgering the members about such issues is nonproductive. I find it useful to take a philosophical approach and embrace the biblical promise, "And we know that God causes all things to work together for good to those who love God, to those who are called according to His purpose" (Romans 8:28).

LOOK FOR NEW TOUR GUIDES

Our tour guide told us Israel's Department of Tourism limits who can serve as an official guide in their country. Certain qualifications and restrictions are carefully set forth and enforced. If you don't qualify, you can't be a guide. They take it very seriously. Yet I don't know if they recruit people to serve as guides or just wait until someone expresses interest.

I don't know about Israeli guides, but I do recommend that you keep your eyes open and identify new recruits to serve as small group leaders. Doing so helps ensure that the groups ministry continues to expand and grow. Besides, developing one or more new leaders adds another exciting dimension to your group's success.

Nurturing new "tour guides" can be accomplished in various ways. Like most factors related to groups, the options are endless. Following are a few ideas to illustrate what I mean.

Co-leader—I participated in several groups in which I shared the group leadership task with another person. Working together and sharing the load, we both served as the group's "official" or designated leader. In one case, I was working with an individual who had little experience leading groups. Even though we were equals in our leadership role, I spent time coaching him on necessary duties and performance. In the end he became an excellent leader.

Apprentice leader—Some group leaders identify a person (or married couple) within or outside their group who has never led a small group but has good potential. The selected individuals are invited to become leaders-in-training by assisting an experienced leader. A plan is devised that gives the apprentice increasing responsibilities until he or she can lead the group without assistance. The ultimate goal is to equip the individual to lead his or her own group, or to equip him or her to do a good job as a permanent assistant leader.

Leadership training—Here again, the options are numerous. However, the basic idea is to design and provide some kind of class or retreat where potential leaders learn basic information about group leadership and gain the necessary confidence to lead a group. Afterwards, follow-up training events can be held on a regular basis to further the leaders' knowledge and skills.

Session leader—An excellent option for training leaders, or to promote shared leadership within the group, is to have members prepare and lead segments within a group meeting. They can lead in prayer, read the Scripture or lesson, guide the discussion, or anything else that permits them to expand their leadership experience. Some people who never thought about leading a group find out they enjoy doing so by participating on this "part-time" basis. Eventually they come to realize they can lead a group on their own.

Potential leaders must meet at least minimal qualifications to serve. The exact qualifications depend on the context and situation. When a church or Christian organization sponsors a group, it often stipulates the requirements necessary for a person to assume group leadership. In some case the requirements are extensive; other times there are few, if any, expectations. Even groups lacking formal sponsorship often have informal, unspoken requirements. Therefore, make certain you know what the requirements are prior to asking someone to consider becoming a group leader.

Your leadership development role can take various paths. At the simplest level all you do is encourage people to talk with your pastor about the leader's role. If you're willing, perhaps you can work with an apprentice leader in your own group. Then after you've led groups for a while, perhaps you will be ready to plan and conduct a small group leaders' training event.

FINAL ADVICE

Just prior to departing on our trip to Israel, some dear friends who had already made the journey shared some advice with me and my family. The insights and suggestions they offered were based on their experience, and their comments proved valuable. Likewise, allow me to share some final words of advice to conclude this book. Helping your group become a real group is possible if you remember to observe the following:

- Depend on the Holy Spirit to give you wisdom and guidance.
- Remain calm; avoid getting upset when you make a mistake.
- Learn from your errors and don't repeat them.
- Find help quickly when you need it.
- Remember that becoming a group is a process that takes time.
- Acknowledge that God is on your side and He wants you to succeed.
- Treat yourself to a whole batch of brownies. You deserve it.

Thanks for taking the time to read this book and learn how you can help your group become a real group. May God bless your group journey.

TAKING ACTION

1. Review the "small group" definition. How does the definition help you better understand what it means to become a "real" group?

2. What kind or type of group are you leading (or do you anticipate leading)? How do you know?

3. Thinking about your group or the potential members of your planned group, which ineffective group behavior pattern (road-block) are you most likely to fall into if the group doesn't watch out? Why?

4. Which option listed among the three "sponsorship" options best describes your group's context? With your answer in mind, explain why you think it's important for your group to "count."

5. Given your groups individual context, describe any external influences that may impact your group.

6. Name someone you think could become a terrific small group leader (like you!). How can you go about approaching this individual and encouraging him or her to consider becoming a leader?

Recommended Resource List

How to Build a Small Groups Ministry
McBride, Neal, F.
NavPress, 1995.
P. O. Box 35001
Colorado Springs, CO 80935

How to Have Great Small Group Meetings
McBride, Neal, F.
NavPress, 1997.
P. O. Box 35001
Colorado Springs, CO 80935

How to Lead Small Groups
McBride, Neal, F.
NavPress, 1990
P. O. Box 35001
Colorado Springs, CO 80935

Learning to Care
Peace, Richard, and Thomas Corrigan.
Pilgrimage/NavPress, 1996.
P. O. Box 35001
Colorado Springs, CO 80935

Author

NEAL MCBRIDE is Dean of Graduate and Continuing Studies at Bethel College in St. Paul, Minnesota. He is a recognized small-group expert and the author of several books, including *How to Lead Small Groups, How to Have Great Small-Groups, How to Have Great Small-Group Meetings,* and *How to Build a Small-Groups Ministry.*

If you liked this book, check out these other titles by Neal McBride!

How to Lead Small Groups

If you've been leading small groups for years or are just beginning, this book will give you the skills you need to be a more effective leader and hit the ground running!

How to Lead Small Groups/$7

How to Build a Small-Groups Ministry

This hands-on workbook gives you the twelve steps you need to develop and administer an effective small-groups ministry. Includes worksheets for creating a specialized ministry for your church.

How to Build a Small-Groups Ministry/$20

How to Have Great Small-Group Meetings

Do your small-group meetings tend to wander off track? Do you often feel unprepared? This book gives you the tools you need to plan and lead small-group meetings that aren't just good—they're great!

How to Have Great Small-Group Meetings/$8

Get your copies today at your local bookstore, or call (800) 366-7788 and ask for offer **#2081**.

Turn your small group from just a bunch of people in to a tightly knit community.

Does your small group feel like just a bunch of people? Do you long for greater intimacy and growth?

With Pilgrimage/NavPress Small-Group Training Seminars you can turn your small group into a community of believers excited to study God's Word and apply it to their lives. With new leadership skills and practical "how to" help, you'll be equipped to provide well-trained leadership and direction for your group, turning it from just a bunch of people in to a community that supports and cares for one another.

Here's what you'll learn.
You'll learn ▶ how trends within society set the stage for small groups ▶ how you can use the four primary phases of group development to guarantee the right fit for every small-group member ▶ seven ways to cultivate a caring atmosphere ▶ five common problems to avoid ▶ the six foundational elements of every small group ▶ and much, much more!

Space is limited. Call (800) GRPS-R-US today for more information about seminars in your area.

(800) 477-7787, ask for offer **#303**

**PILGRIMAGE
NAVPRESS**
www.navpress.org

BIBLE STUDIES AND SMALL-GROUP MATERIALS FROM NAVPRESS

BIBLE STUDY SERIES
Design for Discipleship
Foundation for Christian Living
God in You
Learning to Love
The Life and Ministry of
    Jesus Christ
LifeChange
Love One Another
Pilgrimage Guides
Radical Relationships
Studies in Christian Living
Thinking Through Discipleship

TOPICAL BIBLE STUDIES
Becoming a Woman of Excellence
Becoming a Woman of Freedom
Becoming a Woman of Prayer
Becoming a Woman of Purpose
The Blessing Study Guide
Celebrating Life!
Growing in Christ
Growing Strong in God's Family
Homemaking
Husbands and Wives
Intimacy with God
Jesus Cares for Women
Jesus Changes Women
Lessons on Assurance
Lessons on Christian Living
Loving Your Husband
Loving Your Wife
A Mother's Legacy
Parents and Children
Praying from God's Heart
Strategies for a Successful
    Marriage
Surviving Life in the Fast Lane
To Run and Not Grow Tired
To Stand and Not Be Moved
To Walk and Not Grow Weary

What God Does When Men Pray
When the Squeeze is On

BIBLE STUDIES WITH COMPANION BOOKS
Bold Love
Daughters of Eve
The Discipline of Grace
The Feminine Journey
From Bondage to Bonding
Hiding from Love
Inside Out
The Masculine Journey
The Practice of Godliness
The Pursuit of Holiness
Secret Longings of the Heart
Spiritual Disciplines for the
    Christian Life
Tame Your Fears
Transforming Grace
Trusting God
What Makes a Man?

SMALL-GROUP RESOURCES
201 Great Questions
Discipleship Journal's 101 Best
    Small-Group Ideas
How to Build a Small-Groups
    Ministry
How to Have Great Small-Group
    Meetings
How to Lead Small Groups
The Navigator Bible Studies
    Handbook
New Testament LessonMaker
The Small-Group Leaders
    Training Course

NAVPRESS ◖
BRINGING TRUTH TO LIFE
www.navpress.org

Get your copies today at your local Christian bookstore,
or call (800) 366-7788 and ask for offer **NPBS**.